OF STEAM AND SHEEP
THE STORY OF CRAVEN ARMS

by
Christopher Train

©2000: C.J. Train
Published by Scenesetters
on behalf of Craven Arms Historical Society
with support from Millennium Festival Awards for All
ISBN 1 874200 08 4

**Dedicated to the memory of
John Shipley Clarke (1933 - 2000)**

TABLE OF CONTENTS

Author's Preface 4

1: One Hundred and Fifty Years Ago 5

2: Before Craven Arms 8

3: The Coming of the Railway 16

4: The Development of Craven Arms 28

5: The Life and Times of Craven Arms before 1939 48

6: The Post War Years 63

7: Changing with the Changing Times 71

Index 73

ILLUSTRATIONS

Map of the area around Craven Arms *Inside front cover*
Craven Arms on 1850s Ordnance Survey map 5
Craven Arms Hotel 6
Red Lion Inn at Newton .7
Roman and pre-Roman presence around Craven Arms 8
Stokesay Castle and Church 11
Part of Ogilby's map of Bristol to Chester road 12
Turnpike roads around Craven Arms 13
Milestone (Obelisk) 15
The railways of south Shropshire 17
Craven Arms station c. 1876 with staff 19
Craven Arms station looking south 20
Craven Arms station exterior 21
Goods train from the Central Wales Line 23
Bishop's Castle Railway mixed train c.1930 23
Engine sheds at Craven Arms station 25
Carriage sheds at Craven Arms station 26
1903 25" Ordnance Survey plan 27
Newington Terrace 28
Frontispiece of Temperance Hymn book 31
The Temperance Hotel 31
The lands of the Oldnall Family 33
Market Hall 35
Field names in the Craven Arms area 36
Penlu House, Clun Road .36
Stokesay School, Market Street 41
Stokesay Castle Hotel 44
Corvedale Road 44

Dale Street 45
Newton 45
Market Street 46
Jackson and McCartney's auction yard 46
Date stones on buildings .47
Craven Arms town plan 51
Tradesmen's advertisements from the 1920s 52
Aerial view of Craven Arms station 53
Shrewsbury Cooperative Society's shop, 1912 53
Winter horse sale c.1940 .54
Horse sale catalogue 54
Jackson and McCartney's summer ewe sale 55
1944 ewe catalogue 56
School pupils c.1930 57
Bristol House 58
Fire Brigade 59
Railwaymen's Hut 61
Cricket team 1937 62
Football team 1923 62
Home Guard at Craven Arms station 64
Methodist chapel / Roman Catholic church 65
J.P Wood's shop 67
The station today 68
War memorial (Old Bill) .69
Jackson and McCartney's 1960s summer sale 69
Plan of Craven Arms . . . . *Inside back cover*
The badge of Craven Arms Town Council . . *Back cover*

AUTHOR'S PREFACE

In 1998 the Craven Arms Historical Society decided that for the Millennium year it would produce a new history of Craven Arms to replace the one it had published in 1993. A grant was applied for to help with publication costs and the late John Clarke of Dinchope began the work. Sadly, having assembled a great amount of the necessary material, he became too ill to carry on. In October 1999, a "Millennium Festival Awards for All" grant having been obtained, I was asked to take over the writing of the book with a view to its publication in the first half of 2000. It has been a daunting but fascinating and enjoyable task.

Many people have helped me with it – too many for all to be named individually without stretching this preface to unmanageable length – but some must be mentioned: John Clarke himself for all that he had done before I took over and for having the confidence in my capacity to tackle the book which I initially doubted; his wife, Elizabeth, for assembling and making available John's material, both documentary evidence and photographs, and for giving me access to the minutes of the Stokesay Parochial Church Council; James and Angela Smith and Colin Shiner of the Craven Arms Historical Society for their support and advice; Chris Cannon, the headmaster of Stokesay School, for allowing me to read the School Log Books; the Craven Arms Town Council for agreeing that I might see the Council's minute books and Councillor Neville Stephens and his wife for their hospitality and patience while I read them; the staff of Shropshire Records and Research for their ready response to my requests for documents; Dr Trevor Hill for allowing me to use material from an as yet unpublished article on the *Development of Road Transport in Shropshire with particular reference to the Routes through Craven Arms*; Derek Williams of the Ludlow Historical Research Group for material on the Ludlow Poor Law Union; and last, but by no means least, Mollie Beard, Richard Blakeway, Myfanwy Bourne, Constance Edge, John Glover, Gwilym Jones, Jack Jordan, Connie Jukes, Gladys Jukes, Peter Lyon, John McCartney, Brian Morgan, Arthur Royce, Marjorie Salmon, Brenda Smith, Den Thomas, Mike Wall and Charlie Wood for sharing their memories with me, for giving me the use of documentary material, including photographs, and for enduring my questioning. My thanks to them and to many others with whom I have discussed the past of Craven Arms.

Three more preliminary points are necessary. What follows is what it says it is – The Story of Craven Arms – that is of the settlement which came into being after the railway came in 1852. It deals with the past of Aldon, Halford, Rowton, Sibdon Carwood, Stokesay and Whettleton only to the extent necessary to illuminate its central theme. The history of those places must await another hand. Nor is it a guide book; guides to Stokesay Castle, to the Church, to the Churchyard and to Halford Church are available at those places, and, for those who want to explore the area, *Craven Arms Walks – 10 Walks from Craven Arms* is available from outlets in the town. Lastly, with the amalgamation of the civil parishes of Stokesay and Halford in 1987 the town of Craven Arms came into formal being, although there had been a tendency to refer to it as a town before that time. For ease in writing, I have called it a town throughout.

C. J. Train, Clunbury, May 2000

1: ONE HUNDRED AND FIFTY YEARS AGO

On the morning of 20 April 1852 the first section, from Shrewsbury to Ludlow, of the Shrewsbury and Hereford Railway Company's line to Hereford was ceremonially opened. There was to be a station in the Parish of Stokesay, three hundred yards away from "The Craven Arms Inn", which for the previous fifty years had stood at the junction of the roads north to Shrewsbury, south to Ludlow and Hereford, west to Clun and east to Much Wenlock and Bridgnorth. The station took its name from the Inn, and so, ultimately, gave the name to the place which is the subject of this history.

But to say that the story of Craven Arms begins on that day is true in only a very limited sense. Suggesting that Craven Arms was a railway town, conceived and planned as a consequence of the railway's coming, as if that provides the whole explanation of its location and development, needs elaboration and qualification.

Very little of the present settlement was there in 1852, or, which is more important for understanding its history, for another thirty or more years. And yet what was there in 1852, and especially the pattern of property ownership, was of crucial importance in determining when and how the settlement which we know today was to develop.

The ecclesiastical parishes of Stokesay and Halford, in which Craven Arms now lies, had, in 1851, the year of the most recent census, a population of 673 – Stokesay's being 532 and Halford's 141 – living in 127 dwellings. These were almost entirely agricultural communities – heads of households being in the main farmers or agricultural labourers, or working in related trades, such as wheelwright, blacksmith or lime burner. Their dwellings were scattered in small clusters across the whole of the two parishes. In Stokesay parish there

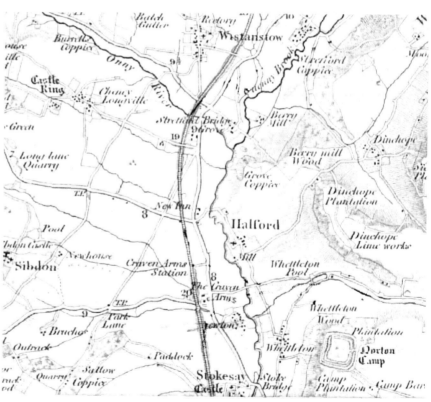

Extract of a 1st edition 1" Ordnance Survey map from about 1855

The Craven Arms Hotel and milestone obelisk

was a small enclave around the Castle and Church at Stokesay, a larger group at Newton, another at Newton Green, close to and including the Craven Arms Inn (together these made up the township of Stoke and Newton), a scatter of properties up Park Lane (the Watling Street, as it climbs away southwards towards View Edge and Rowton), three houses at Rowton, settlements at Aldon, Aldon Gutter, Brandhill (the township of Aldon), and on the east of the River Onny groups of houses at Whettleton Common, Whettleton and Whettleton Pool (the township of Whettleton). In Halford parish, to the east of the river, the pattern was similar – a small settlement around the church, and then scattered houses further east at Dinchope, Moorwood and up on Callow Hill. There were also a few properties in the parish to the west of the river at Newington, where Long Lane, the old coach road from Bishop's Castle and Montgomery, met the Shrewsbury road; these lay in a narrow neck of land which ran westward between Wistanstow parish and Stokesay parish, linking Halford to Sibdon Carwood.

The principal landowners were, in Halford, the Honourable R. H. Clive and, in Stokesay, the Earl of Craven, who held some 1825 acres of the 1935 acres which made up the townships of Stokesay, Newton and Whettleton. But 82 acres in Newton were held by the Oldnall family, and it was this division of ownership in this part of the parish which was to condition the pattern of the development of Craven Arms. The Cravens were, and always had been, absentee landlords, and the larger local farmers, tenants or freeholders, were the leaders in the community – the Church Wardens, Overseers of the Poor, and key members of the Vestry. In Stokesay, they came from all over the parish – there was no focal point geographically, other than the church, which was as much set away from the rest of the community then as it is now. In 1851 the Church Wardens were Francis Bache, a farmer, of Rowton, and Enoch Morris, a farmer, of Stokesay Castle Farm. The Overseers of the Poor were Richard Onians, farmer and innkeeper, of Newton Green, and Richard Beddoes, a farmer, of Rowton. Since the Poor Law Amendment Act of 1834 they, together with the paid Assistant Overseer, had, under the overall control of the Board of Guardians of the Ludlow Poor Law Union, day to day responsibility for looking after the destitute of the parish.

As yet the community had no purpose built school. Schooling in the parish went back to at least 1616, when on his death in that year, Roger Powell left "£10 a year to the poor to be dispensed weekly, the residue to be given towards the maintenance of a schoolmaster to teach the poor children of the Parish of Stokesay". (In the twentieth century the Trust has been used for a scholarship which enabled a child from Stokesay to go to Ludlow Grammar School or Ludlow Girls High School and later to provide books for the school; its future is currently under review.) Until 1839 the children had been taught in the church. A Vestry Meeting was convened in March 1839 "for the purpose of taking into consideration the removal of the present school from the church. The tombs and the church have been much injured by the playful depredations (unavoidably) committed by the children and the church cannot be for any other purpose than its ceremonies and the Divine worship of God, consequently the school must be moved from it and the Parish find a proper place for the school house and having buildings (the late Workhouse), a property belonging to the Parish, we the undersigned do agree to move the school from the church to the late workhouse." Later vestry minutes suggest that this solution was not long pursued (the old workhouse cottage and garden at the bottom of Newton being let as dwellings from 1840 onwards until they were finally sold by the Council in 1998), and in 1851 the school children were, according to Bagshaw's Directory, temporarily being taught in a private house by Joseph Speakes, the schoolmaster appointed in 1847. A vestry minute of August 1850 agreed to pay three years' arrears of rent "for the school room" to Francis Owen, the landlord of the Lion Inn in Newton, who at one stage was also the lessee of what is now 141 Newton. By 1851 the Vestry had set in hand active measures to build a school, which was to be on a site close to the church.

Nor at this time did the community have any other amenities, apart from The Red Lion or Lion in Newton and the Craven Arms Inn, a coaching establishment catering since at least 1810 for the travellers who used the turnpike roads to Ludlow, Shrewsbury, Clun, Bishop's Castle and eastward up the Corvedale. But in the census returns of 1851 is the evidence of a coming event which had been planned for six or more years and which would over the ensuing half century alter the face and, in some respects, the character of this rural and agricultural community. Seven properties – in Newton, Newton Green and Stoke – had, between them, 13 lodgers who were railway labourers (all of whom came from far afield) and one of them, at Stoke Castle, was occupied by Ephraim Clarke, from Towcester in Northamptonshire, and his family, a "Railway Contractor, employing 12 men".

The Red Lion at Newton in the late 19th century

2: BEFORE CRAVEN ARMS

In order to understand why and how the advent of the railway and with it the location of a station at The Craven Arms have had the consequences for the area which they have done, a backward look is necessary before the story can be taken onwards from 1852.

Evidence of man's presence in the area from early times is readily to hand. An earthwork in a field called "Tumpy Field" just past Coton House, the last house on the left of the road out of Craven Arms to Clun (B4368), lying between the road and the Heart of Wales railway, has been identified as a Bronze Age Round Barrow (the second millennium B. C.). And findings of flints, a stone which is not of local origin, on Castle Farm, Stokesay and on the flanks of View Edge also suggest that people were settled here or at least passed this way in even earlier times. Sometime during the period from 600 B.C. down to the time of the Roman invasion of Britain in 43 A.D., settlement hereabouts is attested by Norton Camp, which crowns the hill immediately above and east of Whettleton. This is one of the many Iron Age hill-forts in the area. From exactly when and for how long Norton was occupied cannot be said, but it is virtually certain that it, like most other hill forts in the land, was abandoned after the Romans came.

The Romans reached the middle Marches sometime around 50 A.D., seven or so years after the conquest of Britain under the Emperor Claudius had begun. They were to spend nearly thirty years subduing the tribes of Wales. One of the main strategic roads in the Romans' settlement of the Marches and of Wales ran by Craven Arms. This was the so-called Watling Street West, which linked the legionary fortress at Caerleon in South Wales with the early north-western legionary base at Wroxeter on the Severn just east of Shrewsbury. Two other Roman roads in the area have been proposed. One coming northwards from Gloucester past Leominster and Ludlow ran to the east of Norton Camp (it did not use the Onny Valley) by Dinchope and Stretford

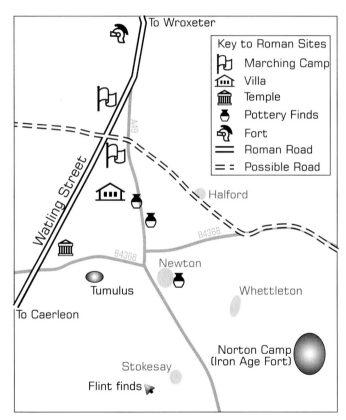

Vicinity of Craven Arms showing evidence of Roman and pre-Roman presence

to join the Watling Street at Marshbrook; the other ran westward from Greensforge, a fort near Dudley, and coming down the Corvedale, crossed the Onny at Newington and headed away into the hills towards Bishop's Castle and onwards to a fort at Fordon Caer on the Severn near Montgomery.

Close to the junction of this road and the Watling Street in Craven Arms and Wistanstow, ample traces of Roman presence have been found. A fort stood on the rising ground above and to the south of the River Onny about 500 metres to the west of the point where the Watling Street crossed the river. This was strategically placed to cover both a river crossing on the main north/south frontier road and one of the routes out of central Wales. Just to the south of it two temporary camps have been identified by aerial photography; these are close to the Watling Street immediately to the west of Newington, and two civilian enclosures, one possibly the precinct of a small Roman Villa and the other said to be reminiscent of a Romano-British temple enclosure, have been found further south and near the line of the Watling Street. Over the years there have also been finds of Roman pottery and of an ornament in and around the town. But none of the finds, in the present state of archaeological knowledge, can be precisely dated nor is there anything suggesting that there was a settlement here on the lines of that at Leintwardine. It was a meeting of ways, but does not appear to have been of sufficient strategic importance or social advantage to warrant any substantial development.

Two further points may be made about the Roman presence here. First, the crossing point of the north/south and east/west routes was well to the north of the present cross roads in the centre of Craven Arms. Secondly neither of the north/south routes which the Romans chose used the valley of the River Onny south of Craven Arms. That circumstance seems to have persisted down to Norman times, since there is evidence from the Domesday Book that the preferred route from Shrewsbury to Hereford when the King came this way was through Leintwardine.

It was not until the making of the Domesday Book, in 1086, – William the Conqueror's monumental record of the land holders of his kingdom at that date and in 1066 – that Stokesay appeared on the pages of history. Before then from the early seventh century this area of England had been part of the Kingdom of Mercia, centred upon Tamworth. The Dyke, called after the Mercian King Offa, built soon after 784 to mark the frontier between his territories and those of the Welsh kingdoms, remains an impressive monument to the Mercians' control of this land (its line across southern Shropshire in the Clun Valley runs some fifteen miles to the west of Craven Arms). The other principal manifestation of Saxon settlement is to be found in place names – typically those ending in 'ton' – a settlement – and 'bury' – a fortified place or, more probably in this area, a manor house: Sibdon – the settlement of Sibba (a person's name); Aston – the settlement to the East (Aldon, on the other hand, means the hill with a spring); and Diddlebury – the manor of Dudela (a personal name). Less prominent, because Saxon churches were generally built of wood and have not survived, are the traces of Saxon stonework in local churches. Two of the best examples in Shropshire are close to Craven Arms at St. Peter, Diddlebury and St. Peter, Stanton Lacy.

Stokesay, then known simply as Stoke (a dependent settlement), was held in late Saxon times by Aldred. It was a medium sized manor for the area, having in 1086 land sufficient for 14 ploughs, smaller than Clun (60 ploughs), Lydbury North (about 100 ploughs) and Stanton Lacy (50 ploughs), and comparable with Hopesay (14 ploughs) and Wistanstow (15 ploughs). 20 villagers were there, 9 female cottagers and 16 slaves, male and female. There was also a mill, thought to have stood upstream from Stokesay Bridge, which paid nine packloads of wheat to the lord, a miller and, an unusual entry, a beekeeper. The manor was valued at £10 before 1066, but no later value was given. In 1086 it was held by Roger de Lacy. He had substantial holdings along the Marches, principally in Herefordshire, but also, in Shropshire, the large and valuable manor of Stanton Lacy, in the southern corner of which the Lacys built Ludlow Castle, and the manors of Aldon (of a similar size to Stokesay), Stokesay and Stoke upon Tern in the north of the county – in early days these were distinguished as South and North Stoke.

Sibdon Carwood, a small manor with sufficient land for three ploughs, gains notice in the Lordship of Picot de Say – Lord of Clun. Like Clunbury, Coston, Edgton and Kempton it had been held before the Conquest by a man called Swein. Newton, Whettleton, Halford and Dinchope were not mentioned. Some scholars have speculated that the two latter may have been an otherwise unidentified manor, called Chinbaldescote, belonging to St. Mary's Church, Bromfield. Halford and Dinchope were later an estate held by the Priors of Bromfield, the chapel being an ancient but detached chapelry of the parish of Bromfield until 1841, when it became a separate parish, its living held in conjunction with the living of Sibdon Carwood. The names Newton and Whettleton (in different forms) first appear in documents a hundred or so years later than the Domesday Book, but the settlements seem to be part of the Stokesay Manor. When they were first settled cannot be said – their 'ton' suffixes suggest they may have been of Saxon origin.

Early in the twelfth century and for some hundred years until about 1240 the family of de Say, probably a branch connected with Picot de Say the Domesday Lord of Clun, held the Lacy manors of North Stoke and South Stoke as undertenants of the Lacys. It is at the end of this period in 1255 that the name "Stoke Say" first appears. When the male Lacy line ceased in 1241, Stokesay passed to John de Verdon, the husband of the younger of the Lacy heiresses and he is described as "Lord of Stoke Say, Wetliton and Neuton" in 1255.

But earlier than this the de Says had made endowments to Haughmond Abbey, near Shrewsbury, not only of Stokesay Church but also of the mill and of pieces of land in Newton, and the Abbey acquired further land there in the last years of the thirteenth century. Around that time William Dun sold the Abbey 3fi acres in the fields of Newton in several small parcels, which were distinguished from land belonging to Hugh de Say, while Hugh himself gave half an acre "between the abbot's land and David Hordrit's in the field above Newton village, and an acre of meadow between Hancforde bridge [that is, perhaps, Halford Bridge] and the abbot's grange [that is the Abbey's Grange Farm]". Where all the various pieces of land and the grange were cannot be certainly said, but there must be a strong supposition that when the Abbey's lands were confiscated at the dissolution of the monasteries in the sixteenth century they went not to the then Lord of Stokesay but to some other person. This would explain why, in 1841, when the Tithe Apportionment was made, the Earl of Craven was not the sole land owner in the Parish and land "above Newton village" was in the hands of another owner.

The date at which a house was first built on the site of Stokesay Castle (it was not, in fact, known as Stokesay Castle until much later and is better described as a fortified manor house) is unknown, but it is to be supposed that the de Says had a dwelling there from Norman times. The present buildings, apart from the gatehouse, which dates from the mid-seventeenth century, were built during the second half of the thirteenth century, a principal contributor to their development being the wealthy wool merchant, Lawrence de Ludlowe, into whose family's hands the estate had come by 1281, and who, in 1291, obtained from Edward I the licence to crenellate his house at Stokesay, that is to provide it with battlements and "walls of lime and stone". The country residence of a wealthy and powerful man needed to be adequately protected in this area and at this time – it was not merely a symbol of his standing. For much of the thirteenth century the Central Marches had been the scene of armed conflict and even

Stokesay Castle and Church

though Edward I had in the 1280s at last brought the Welsh to heel and peace to the Marches, Welsh raiding parties were continuing to make their presence felt in South Shropshire in the early fourteenth century. Sometime around 1306 a number of local townships, including Peaton, Burwarton and Horderley sought relief from taxes because they had been "burnt, plundered and destroyed by the Welsh". The defensive arrangements at Stokesay, with moat and sturdy walls, though not sufficient to withstand an organised siege, were adequate to hold off this kind of casual raider, and to stand ward at the head of the narrow valley through which one of the north/south routes along the Marches now passed.

There is no mention of a church at Stokesay in the Domesday Book, but it was certainly in existence by the 1170s when Hugh de Say gave it to Haughmond Abbey, in whose charge it remained until the dissolution of the monasteries in 1539. The present church, dedicated to St John the Baptist, was largely rebuilt in 1654, but the nave may represent the ground plan of the earlier church and there are Norman shafts and capitals in the south porch.

The Stokesay estate remained with the Ludlows for 200 years. Ten generations were there down to the end of the fifteenth century. It then passed through several hands before being acquired in 1620 by the Craven Family, Dame Elizabeth Craven and her son, William. Dame Elizabeth was the widow of Sir William Craven, a Yorkshireman of humble origins who had come to London and made a fortune in the drapery trade. His son, William, a soldier of fortune with close connections to the Stuarts, was ennobled in 1627, taking the name of Baron Craven of Hampstead Marshall, another of the newly acquired family estates, in West Berkshire near Newbury. The Cravens never resided in Shropshire and, probably soon after their purchase of Stokesay, it was let on a long lease to Charles Baldwyn of Elsich nearby in the parish of Diddlebury.

Shortly thereafter Stokesay played a small part in the events of the English Civil War. Early in the summer of 1645 a Parliamentary force from Shrewsbury took the Castle, which, like a number of others in the area, was being held for the King. A mere show of force was sufficient to secure its surrender. But in the June of that year Sir Michael Woodhouse, the Royalist commander at Ludlow, attempted to reassert the King's control in south-west Shropshire. In a battle fought most probably on the sloping land above the Onny by Whettleton he was routed and barely escaped with his own life, losing substantial amounts of equipment and many soldiers and officers. Once Parliament's control of the country was secured, Stokesay was ordered to be slighted, but, for some reason, only the curtain wall was demolished, in 1647. However sometime in

the War, whether during the events of 1645 or later, Stokesay Church was so badly damaged – it is described as being "burnt down in the late calamitous time" – that it required total rebuilding. In the Church on the tower arch there is an inscription: AN. DOM. 1654. THIS CHURCH WAS REBUILT BY THE PIOUS OVERSIGHT OF GEORGE POWELL GENT. AND GEORGE LAMBE, CHURCHWARDENS. THIS ARCH WAS GIVEN BY JOHN CHESHIRE JOYNER.

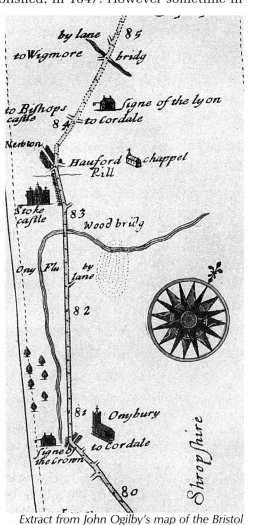

Extract from John Ogilby's map of the Bristol to Chester road, 1675

After the Civil War the Baldwyns continued to live at Stokesay until the end of the century, the last member to do so, from 1683, being another Charles Baldwyn. The Castle then became unoccupied and fell gradually into disrepair, being used as outbuildings for the nearby Castle Farm. But the church, which lay close to the geographical centre of the parish, remained the focus of the parish's administrative activity, even though the nearest and long standing settlements, Newton and Whettleton, were some distance away.

From the late seventeenth century maps begin to give a picture of the lie of the land. They have to be treated with care, since, until the beginning of the nineteenth century, accuracy of survey or reproduction cannot always be relied upon. Nevertheless, it may with some confidence be said, relying upon John Ogilby's map of the Bristol to Chester road in 1675, that the main road north from Ludlow came up from Onibury, crossing the Onny by a wooden bridge at Stokesay, through Newton, where it is shown as crossing a "rill" – the small stream which, running behind Newton to the west, joins the Onny just to its south – and on to Church Stretton and Shrewsbury, with a left turn at Newington up Long Lane to Bishop's Castle. An earlier route may have avoided the Onny crossing at Stokesay and gone up the eastern side of the valley through Whettleton to Halford (the link between Whettleton and the road to Halford is now marked by a footpath), crossing the

Onny at Newington to link with the Bishop's Castle road and the road north.

In the 1750s the turnpike system came to this part of Shropshire. The Turnpike Acts were intended to improve the country's roads by placing the burden of maintaining, and in some instances making, the main roads upon the Turnpike Trusts, who gained their finances from tolls paid by the travellers on the roads, rather than relying, often ineffectually, upon the local communities through which the roads passed to keep them in an adequate state. Two Acts, of 1756 (Second Ludlow Trust) and 1768 (Bishop's Castle Trust), converted the principal roads through Stokesay parish to turnpikes. The first dealt with the road from Ludlow to Church Stretton (the modern A49) and a number of roads up the Corvedale. What is now Craven Arms was linked with the roads in the Corvedale (an Act of the same year brought the road south-westward from Much Wenlock to the Corvedale into this system). The 1768 Act turnpiked the roads from Clun to Craven Arms (B4368), from Bishop's Castle to Newington through Edgton, and from Bishop's

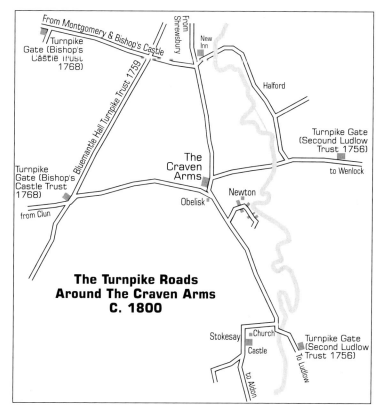

The Turnpike Roads Around The Craven Arms C. 1800

Castle to Craven Arms through Lydbury North, Kempton and Little Brampton (B4385). An Act of 1759 turnpiked the Watling Street southward from Wistanstow. There were toll gates on the road from Ludlow just before the turn to Whettleton, on the road to Wenlock at Whettleton Pool, at the junction of the Clun road and the Watling Street, and on Long Lane.

It is easy to overstate the poor condition of the country's roads before the Turnpike Acts, since people and goods have moved around the land from time immemorial and there were developed coaching and, particularly, carrying trades well before the middle of the eighteenth century. There can, however, be little doubt both that the state of many roads in winter made travel difficult, and, conversely, that the turnpike system brought with it a substantial improvement in the carriage of people, of mail and of goods. And this was in the longer term to play a part in the development of the settlement which became Craven Arms.

Trade directories provide information about Shropshire coach services, whose routes would have brought them by Newton Green. In 1801 'The New Post-Coach' ran northwards from Hereford to Shrewsbury on Tuesdays and Fridays and southwards on Sundays and Wednesdays. In 1811 Felton's Description of the Town of Ludlow records "The PRINCE REGENT COACH from Mountford's Holyhead Office, Shrewsbury, every Sunday, Wednesday and Friday mornings at 6 o'clock, arrives at the Crown Inn, Ludlow, same mornings at 11 o'clock, and returns to Shrewsbury same days at 1 o'clock." While "The DEFIANCE COACH sets out from the Angel Inn, Ludlow, every Sunday, Tuesday, and Thursday, at 12 o'clock in the forenoon; arrives at the Lion Inn, Shrewsbury, the same evening; starts from thence every Monday, Wednesday and Friday mornings at 6 o'clock, and arrives in Ludlow the same mornings at 11 o'clock." In 1835 The Defiance left The Talbot Inn, Shrewsbury daily for Hereford at 12 midday with The Alert departing from The Lion at 1 p.m. Also passing through Newton Green was The Dart on a twice weekly service from Aberystwyth to Kidderminster via Bishop's Castle and Ludlow.

A mail coach service along the Shrewsbury/Hereford road does not seem to have started until the early nineteenth century. In 1793 the entry for Church Stretton in The Universal British Directory records "There is no regular post. A newsman from Salop passes through every Friday to Ludlow and returns to Salop on Saturday night, who generally brings the letters." There had been a mail coach running into Shrewsbury from London since 1785 and there was a thrice weekly mail coach from London to Ludlow, so the newsman from Shrewsbury could have picked up letters from both ends of his route. But by 1811 a mail coach from The Angel Inn, Ludlow was running to Shrewsbury three times a week, on Monday, Wednesday and Friday, and in May that year a mail service from Ludlow to Aberystwyth during the bathing season (Aberystwyth being a fashionable seaside resort at this time) ran via Bishop's Castle, Montgomery, Newtown, Llanidloes and Devil's Bridge. By the late 1820s there was a daily Royal Mail route from Shrewsbury to Hereford and Bristol, and this linked at Shrewsbury with routes to London, Chester, Holyhead and into mid-Wales, and at Ludlow to London through Tenbury and Worcester.

Alongside the passenger and mail services the carrying trade was also developing. By 1785 a carrier called Taylor ran a weekly service from London to Bishop's Castle, leaving "The George Inn" in West Smithfield in London on a Saturday evening, and by 1788 two other waggons were on this route, leaving London on Mondays and Fridays. In 1793 it was reported for Bishop's Castle that "Taylor's waggon from 'The George', Smithfield and 'The Green Man and Still', Oxford St. every Sunday, comes in here every Saturday; returns the same evening." In 1811 Felton's Description of Ludlow reported "ROBERT'S Bishop's Castle Waggon goes every Sunday morning, and returns on Monday. MAXON'S Manchester Waggon arrives at his Warehouse, Corve Street, Ludlow, on Wednesday; goes out next morning to Leominster with goods for Hereford, Brecknock, Monmouth and all South Wales; returns to Ludlow the same night, and sets out on Friday morning for Shrewsbury, Chester, and Manchester....A man arrives with Eddowes's Salopian Journal at 7 o'clock every Wednesday evening....A cart arrives at the Compasses Inn, with Wood & Watton's Shrewsbury Chronicle every Friday evening and returns the following morning." By 1822 the Manchester service had increased to twice a week and two other carriers were operating through Newton Green, Roberts and Clewer, who linked Bishop's Castle to London, via Ludlow on a Monday, and Francis Durnall who linked Shrewsbury to Ludlow on a Friday. These services increased in the 1830s and 1840s, and by 1842 there was a twice weekly service from Shrewsbury to South Wales via Hereford on Mondays and Thursdays and another from Shrewsbury to Hereford on Thursdays and Saturdays. Additionally Bishop's Castle was linked to Ludlow on

Mondays, and there were services between Shrewsbury and Ludlow on Wednesdays and Thursdays and two on Saturdays. In the 1850s two local carriers were operating between Ludlow and Stokesay, Thomas Colton on a Monday, Thursday and Saturday and John Humphries on a Monday. But, as with the stage and mail coaches, their days were to be numbered.

Travellers and carriers on the roads and their horses needed sustenance and service, and a New Inn, at the junction of the roads to Shrewsbury and Bishop's Castle by Long Lane is shown in a map of about 1710. It was still there when the first Ordnance Survey map was being surveyed just before 1820, but by 1840 the Tithe Apportionment Map describes it as a house, garden and fold (the later Newington Farm). There was also an Inn in Newton, The Lion or The Red Lion, held on lease from the Earl of Craven, which had been there since at least 1768 and perhaps earlier. (Ogilby's Map of 1655 showed "The Sign of the Lion" on the site of the New Inn and not at Newton, but that may be a mistake.)

Sometime between 1772 and 1822 the road from Ludlow to Shrewsbury to the north of Stokesay was diverted to by-pass Newton. In the former year Matthias Baker's detailed map of the Manor of Stokesay showed the road up from Ludlow passing through the settlement of Newton, but, when Thomas Telford replaced the old bridge at Stokesay, which had been swept away by a great flood in December 1821, his plan shows the road on its present line (he had moved the bridge further north – it had originally been below the weir – straightening a substantial meander in the stream just above this point). Perhaps the diversion of the road was associated with the establishment of the Craven Arms Inn which is mentioned in Robert Baugh's Map of Shropshire in 1808 but does not appear in 1772; the 1901 Return of Licensed Houses stated that it received its licence in 1810. It was built on the Earl of Craven's land – the Craven Estate papers in the Bodleian Library throw no light on its date – at the junction of the main road north to Shrewsbury and the turnpike road from Clun (which could also be used to reach Bishop's Castle on an easier route than that over the hills through Edgton) and close to the turnpike road eastward to Wenlock and Bridgnorth. It was described in 1851 as a "handsome and commodious hotel, not surpassed by any in the county", having 15 bedrooms and stabling for 30 horses. With its milestone obelisk opposite giving the distances to many of the principal towns in the country, it was clearly built specifically to cater for an increasing trade on the roads by which it stood.

That trade was, however, very soon to be diverted to another route.

The milestone outside the Craven Arms Hotel epitomises the heyday of the coaching era

3: THE COMING OF THE RAILWAY

On 3 August 1846 the Act enabling the Shrewsbury and Hereford Railway to be built was passed. Its stated purposes were to provide a link between South and North Wales and the Mersey, and to facilitate local trade. But in the immediately following years the money market was depressed and there was a general depreciation in the value of railway property. In consequence the Shrewsbury and Hereford Railway Company experienced serious difficulty in raising the money necessary to finance their project. It was kept alive by the determination of the Company's Chairman, Mr W. Ormsby-Gore M. P., and by the ingenuity of the engineer, Henry Robertson, in cutting costs. The original estimate of cost, when Mr. Ormsby-Gore and the Hon. R. H. Clive gave evidence to the House of Lords Committee in July 1846, was £796,904 for construction and £93,991 for land. By June 1850 those estimates were reduced to £503,804 and £60,000 respectively. Approval was obtained in August 1848 to extend the statutory powers for the line from their original terminal date of August 1849. During 1849 lines opened from Shrewsbury to Chester and to Birmingham (Mr. Ormsby-Gore was on the board and at one time Chairman of both of these Companies). On 3 December 1850 orders were given for the work on the line to Hereford to begin. Among others Lord Craven and the Hon. R. H. Clive agreed to take the whole value of their land in shares. Thomas Brassey, one of the great Victorian Railway builders, was engaged as contractor, on the condition that he should have the first lease of the railway.

Once the work had begun the contractor pressed on hard. A newspaper account in 1851 of an exploratory trip along the line to view the work reported progress as follows:

"Notwithstanding the work here [south of Marshbrook] is of a very formidable nature, the great barriers are fast disappearing before the brawny arms of experienced British workmen, many of whom are from the green isle. There is also a heavy piece of work at the Grange in Condover parish. This is the largest though not the deepest cutting on the line. The labour here, as well as at Leebotwood, is going on night and day, so anxious are the company to have the line opened from Shrewsbury to Ludlow at the specified time. We have heard that there are 1,500 to 2,000 men employed on the works, and from three to four hundred horses; taking this fact into consideration we cannot wonder at the rapid and extremely satisfactory way in which this great undertaking is being completed....We are confident, from what we have witnessed, and from the able and energetic way in which the works are being carried on, that if the weather continues favourable the authorities connected with this line will be able to make good their stipulation, namely to have the line opened at (or about) Christmas."

The writer went on: "At the Craven Arms the line intersects the road from Bishop's Castle to Ludlow. Here, therefore, there will be a station of considerable importance, as it will be a point of approach to railway conveyance, for passengers and goods traffic, for a long line of country in this and the neighbouring counties of Radnorshire and Montgomeryshire." It was this geographical circumstance, then, which led to the site close to the Craven Arms Inn being chosen for a station in this area, rather than further north near the village of Wistanstow, whose inhabitants, despite repeated refusals – "The Craven Arms Station being so close to the village of Wistanstow" – , continued to petition the Company for a station throughout 1852. This tells against the local memory that the station was originally planned to have been south of Stokesay Castle. It would have been both closer to Onibury station than the usual spacing of stations on main routes dictated and inconveniently far from the road junctions which gave access to the hinterland.

In the event the Christmas deadline was not met. On 18 March 1852 two engines with 40 wagons tested the rails from Shrewsbury to Ludlow. Leaving Ludlow at 4 o'clock on the return journey, they made a stop at Craven Arms. Mr. George Finley, 'the conductor of the second engine' had "ordered, on going up, a dinner at Mr Onian's of the Craven Arms Inn for the sub-contractors and their friends on return. The dinner was bountiful and served up in a very superior manner; the wines were excellent and port, sherry and champagne were freely circulated." There were, as was customary on these occasions, numerous toasts and speeches.

But the great celebrations were reserved for the Railway's opening. Eddowes's Journal of Wednesday 21 April 1852 reported: "The morning of yesterday, Tuesday 20th, opened a new era to the inhabitants of Ludlow and the district adjoining the line. Shortly before eleven a special train arrived [at Shrewsbury] from Chester with a party from that city and neighbourhood. Thirty five coaches, qualified to hold about 200 persons, drew up on the line about half past eleven o'clock, steamed by two splendid engines, bearing flags, and in a few minutes the whole company were seated and the train started amid the cheers of the passengers and people. There was a battery of cannon

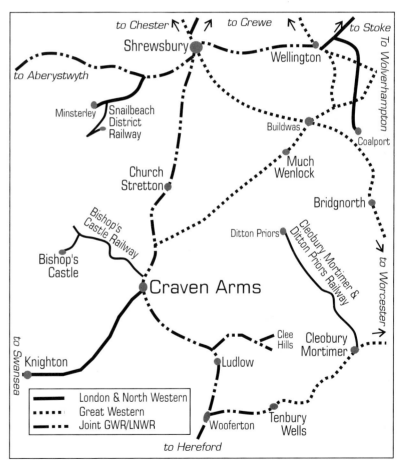

The Railways of South Shropshire

on a truck at the end of the train, from which a volley was fired as it started, and these with the ringing of bells and the strains of the music contributed to form a most splendid ensemble."

The journey south is described in detail, and then: "Just before we approached Craven Arms the bridge over the line was most tastefully decked with flags and evergreens and on each side 'Success'. The place was here on the *qui vivre* and opposite the station at which we stopped about eight minutes were triumphant arches and festoons of evergreens, and also a band. The Inn at Craven Arms and the Castle at Stoke displayed a number of flags. The run from Church Stretton to Craven Arms occupied twenty minutes."

Eddowes also offered a description of the places through which the railway ran. "We then proceed to the Craven Arms, a large, commodious and first-rate posting establishment, surrounded by extensive and picturesque scenery. At this place there is a large and commodious station, in the Elizabethian *[sic]* style of architecture, with rich pointed gables, a large booking office, ladies' and gentlemen's waiting rooms, an excellent residence, railway and road weighing machine, sidings, turn-tables, a platform of 170 feet in length, cattle landing, 200 feet, goods warehouse, 80 ft. by 40, coal wharf, etc." In contrast, Church Stretton station was "in the modern English Villa style".

When the train arrived at Ludlow there were great festivities; at the Assembly Rooms "The boar's head which formed a conspicuous object at the centre table had affixed to it a neatly executed label on which was written 'Shrewsbury and Hereford Railway, opened to Ludlow April 20th 1852'. The tout ensemble which was produced was exceedingly pleasing." But Craven Arms, if less flamboyant, was not to be outdone.

Eddowes's local correspondent reported: "In the afternoon of Tuesday a public dinner in celebration of the opening of the railway was held at the well-known Craven Arms about seven miles from Ludlow. Previous to the arrival of the train a large number of persons were assembled at this spot from the adjacent villages and also from Bishop's Castle, Knighton and other distant places, and during the remainder of the day the scene near the Inn was more like a Fair than anything else. The rooms of the house were completely crowded and the demand for victuals and liquor most extensive. The Newton Band, which had been expressly engaged, played many favourite airs, marches, polkas, etc. in excellent style. About half past five o'clock a numerous company sat down to dinner under the presidency of R. Green esq. of Knighton, F. Bach esq. of Rowton officiating as vice-chairman. The dinner was served up in Mr. and Mrs. Onian's proverbially liberal and tasty style – the wines were exceedingly good, and the dessert ample and choice. Upon the withdrawal of the cloth..." there were a number of protracted speeches and associated toasts, together with the occasional song and glee.

Among those toasted was Mr. Walker "their station master, who was present. Most of those around the table would, no doubt, be brought into contact with Mr. Walker, officially and otherwise; no doubt he would acquit himself creditably. He had most important interests committed to his charge, and would have to deal with various characters; but being chosen for the situation he holds no doubt he has been well-recommended and therefore it may safely be anticipated that all persons will meet with proper civility and attention from his hands at the station. (Hear.) He trusted Mr. Walker would always do his duty to others and they to him. He had pleasure in proposing 'The health of Mr. Walker, the station master'. (Prolonged cheering.)"

In reply "Mr. Walker hoped that, though he was a stranger amongst them at present, he should be better acquainted in a few months. His duties as station master would be devoted to giving satisfaction to those with whom he had business. He sincerely thanked the chairman for so kindly proposing and the company for drinking his health. (Cheers.)" "The Chairman next proposed 'The navvies on Mr. Clarke's contract' speaking in high terms of their orderly conduct." He also gave the 'agricultural labourers'. A glee 'Hail, smiling morn' intervened before a toast to 'prosperity to the Newspaper Press of this country'. "The chairman vacated the chair, which was taken by Mr. F. Bach, and the conviviality of the evening continued for some time longer. The Newton band was stationed near the door and played a variety of pieces during the evening.

"Ere we conclude our remarks in reference to this undertaking there are still remaining two or three circumstances connected with the construction of the line which cannot fail to interest our readers. For instance, the Parliamentary estimate for constructing it was about £20,000 per mile; nevertheless by the excellent scheming adopted, and the minute calculations made, as well as the experience and ingenuity brought to bear on the survey by the engineers, and by altering the curves and gradients, the cuttings and embankments have been reduced about a half; hence the difference in expense being diminished from £20,000 to about £8,000 per mile. We very much question whether the Shrewsbury and Hereford Railway would ever have been commenced, if the work had not been curtailed to the extent as above stated; consequently all who are interested in the success of this line must feel deeply indepted [sic] to those gentlemen (the engineers) for their ingenuity, consummate skill, and untiring perseverance in enabling the shareholders and all concerned to carry out the construction of it, which must eventually prove an inestimable boon not only to the towns but also to the agricultural and mineral districts through which it passes, as well as the inhabitants of the contiguous country; and from the telling circumstance just referred to, we cannot but think that, at no very distant period, it must undoubtedly prove a profitable speculation to those enterprising individuals who have embarked their capital in this greatly desired undertaking."

So began the story of the railway through The Craven Arms. Business got speedily under way. The Shrewsbury Chronicle gave a timetable with three trains each way in the first week and there were soon five trains a day in each direction: to Ludlow at 6.40 a.m., 9.56 a.m., 1.55 p.m., 5.05 p.m. and 8.06 p.m., and to Shrewsbury at

The station staff assembled for a photograph, with a train probably bound for Knighton in about 1876

4.40 a.m., 8 a.m., 11.30 a.m., 3.45 p.m. and 6.46 p.m. The journey time to Ludlow was about 20 minutes and to Shrewsbury about an hour. The early afternoon train to Ludlow connected with the Hereford stage coach, as did the late morning train from Ludlow. It was possible to leave Craven Arms for Shrewsbury at 8 o'clock in the morning and to be in London, via Stafford, at 4 o'clock in the afternoon. The reverse journey meant a 10 o'clock departure from London arriving at Craven Arms at five minutes past five, either via Stafford or Birmingham. Merchandise trains left Shrewsbury at 5 a.m. and 12.30 p.m. and Ludlow at 8.15 a.m. and 4.30 p m. each day. At the May Board meeting of the Company the Secretary said that the first ten days of running had produced £559. 13s 3d [£559.67] receipts, and the local newspaper reported that "upwards of 1,000 tons of coal have passed per rail from 21st of April to the 1st of May inclusive. This augurs well for the line." Mr. Brassey's handbill, advertising the opening of the line on 20 April, had stated that after that date "coals (of every description), lime, slates, etc. may be had at all stations at moderate prices."

But all was not well at The Craven Arms station, which was being manned by John Walker (at a salary of 20/- [£1] a week), a porter and a goods porter (both on 12/- [60p] a week). Mr. Walker, so warmly welcomed two months previously, had, it was reported to the Board on 26 June, been suspended for deficiencies in his accounts and loss of about 50 bags of Guano [manure] from the warehouse. "Mr. Walker is not suspected of wilfully making away with the property, but has been neglectful and careless of the trust reposed in him." It was ordered that in consideration of a favourable report to the Board from the inhabitants of the Craven Arms (this is the earliest reference to Craven Arms as a place) and Parish of Wistanstow Mr Walker was allowed further time to discover where the missing guano had gone and to explain the other deficiencies in his accounts. Walker explained himself to the Board, but on 4 August he was transferred to Dorrington – a demotion – and Mr. Gawain Clarke was appointed to Craven Arms. The wretched Walker did not survive long at Dorrington; having been absent from duty since 26 October, he was replaced on 10 November and left the Company's service.

Craven Arms was one of three stations later (in 1856) designated as 1st class on the line, the others being Ludlow and Leominster (after the opening of the line through to Hereford in December 1853 – the construction of Dinmore Tunnel being the cause of the delay),Wooferton and

Craven Arms station looking south

G.M. Perkins

• 20 •

Church Stretton 2nd Class, Marshbrook and Dorrington 3rd Class and the rest 4th class; these included, on the section north of Ludlow, Bromfield, Onibury, Leebotwood and Condover. By 1857 the pay for a station master at a first class station, reflecting the receipts at the stations, had almost doubled from its original £52 a year to £100. The station master was required to be proficient in the use of the electric telegraph.

Craven Arms station exterior

The increase in pay also reflected an increase in the size of the railway facilities at Craven Arms. In less than a year, on 30 March 1853, the Board noted the need for further accommodation for goods. Two years later a shed was requested for storing guano and other merchandise, and stabling for horses (some of these may have been used for shunting). In October 1856 there was an extension to the sidings, Mr. Dicken of the Chirk Castle Colliery having applied for a coal wharf. And there was further extension of goods facilities in November 1860. More staff were being recruited over these years – a booking clerk, a gate keeper at the Craven Arms crossing (the level crossing lodge was completed in 1856) who became the pointsman in charge of the nearby distant signal, a goodswarehouseman, a goods clerk and an additional goods porter. In addition to the use of the route for the transport of coal and iron ore from South Wales to the north-west (the line from Hereford to Newport opened in 1854), a variety of other goods were being carried. Smythe Brothers of Liverpool sought leave to stack bark at the station – for the tanning industry. The loss of a bag of clover seed led to a claim against the Company by a Bishop's Castle farmer, and the Company also had to pay for the non-delivery of a barrel of beer also destined for Bishop's Castle and for delay and damage to a load of skins. John Ford, a warehouseman, was accused of negligence in weighing poultry, while William Haines, a supplementary porter, appeared before the Ludlow Magistrates in March 1856 for stealing brandy from the cache at the station. The growth in timber carrying required the provision of more wagons in 1860.

Kelly's Directory for 1863 recorded three coal merchants at Craven Arms Station, George Doody, William Field and John Morgan. By 1870 Morgan had gone, to be replaced by Richard Atfield and Co. ("also at Ludlow"), and Thornley and Sons, timber merchants, had a depot there.

Another contemporary source reveals not only how busy the station at Craven Arms quickly became but also the benefits that the railway could bring to the rural communities which it served. This comes from the evidence given to the House of Lords Committee in May 1861 in support of the Bishop's Castle Railway (the original Act of 1861 was for making a railway to link the Oswestry and Newtown Railway near Montgomery to the Shrewsbury and Hereford Railway near Craven Arms, with branches to Montgomery and to Bishop's Castle).

The first witness was the Reverend John Bright of Totterton, the Vicar of Lydbury North and a substantial landowner (about 1,400 acres) and farmer in the area. He got his lime for his fields from near Llanymynech – the railway would cut the cost by half, saving a £100 a year on a farm of 300 acres. But guano was brought from London by water to Newport and thence by rail on the Shrewsbury and Hereford Railway, as a later witness – John Morgan, a dealer in lime, coals, slate and artificial manures, with a depot at the Craven Arms Station – testified. This and coal (from Staffordshire) came up by road from Craven Arms Station at considerable cost. Of outgoing items, timber went to Craven Arms by land carriage in very considerable quantities. "What" the Reverend Bright was asked, "are the roads like to Craven Arms Station?" "They are very bad roads in the winter," was the reply. "And unfortunately the chief part of the timber is carried in the winter and it has been almost impossible to keep them in passable order – we had ruts broken up this winter on the roads 9 to 10 inches deep." "They are cut up by the number of teams that ply them?" "Yes. Very much cut up – a great increase of traffic in timber has taken place in recent years." The chief markets for stock were identified as Dudley, Bilston, Birmingham and Walsall, but a great many animals went south to Worcester and Gloucester. At present they were driven to Craven Arms. Summing up, Counsel for the prospective railway company put it to the Reverend Bright as follows: "The Craven Arms is a very important station, is it not – it is a sort of central railway depot, I believe." "Yes." "And likely to become still more important? "Yes. It is at the meeting of five roads and it is likely to be a very great centre."

James Tomlins, a miller, of Snead, said that he bought his grain from Hereford (10,000 bushels in the previous six months). It took a team 12 to 13 hours to cart the grain the 11 miles – a two hour ride by horse – from Craven Arms Station, at a cost of 8/- [40p] a ton. He confirmed the bad state of the roads. Thomas Williams, a Montgomery farmer, describing the importance of the Bishop's Castle Fair, revealed how the railway had affected the cattle trade. In 1852 one man bought upwards of £4,000 of stock at Bishop's Castle Fair "to come down to the inland markets". Before the Hereford and Shrewsbury line was opened they were driven by road over the Clee Hills towards Bridgnorth and Wolverhampton. There they diverged according to the different markets they were going to. Now they went down to Craven Arms and onto the train. But there was also an incoming cattle trade: "Their Lordships are aware that down the Vale of Severn there is very valuable and rich feeding country on which I feed myself and many others. I have to travel to Hereford and Leominster and Knighton to buy poor stock and at present I have no means of trucking the stock, but by taking it round by Shrewsbury or coming to the Craven Arms and there taking them out of the trucks, which is very injurious to them, and driving them to Montgomery." Williams agreed with the other witnesses that Craven Arms was a very important station and railway depot, which was already much crowded with traffic of different descriptions.

The Bishop's Castle Railway was, however, not the first additional line proposed to make a junction with the Shrewsbury and Hereford Railway at Craven Arms. A scheme for a link through mid-Wales to south-west Wales had been on the stocks since 1854. Eddowes's Journal of Wednesday 25 August 1858 reported: "Unfortunately the monetary derangements of the country and the breaking out of the Russian War interfered with further progress of the scheme [after 1854] and it was wisely deferred until a more fitting opportunity offered. The project was kept in abeyance until last year, when active steps were taken to bring it before public notice. Instead, however, of proceeding with the whole line it was determined to apply for powers to construct a portion of it only, from Craven Arms to Knighton. This application was successful and in May last we had the pleasure of informing our readers that the first link in the great chain of communication remaining to be completed between Manchester and Milford Haven [then planned to be a major port for the Atlantic and American trade] had received the sanction of Parliament." The

From the 1860s to 1960s large volumes of livestock and goods passed through Craven Arms from the Central Wales line to Knighton, Llandrindod Wells and Swansea

first sod on the new railway had been cut at Knighton a week before this report and work was pressed ahead by the contractors, Brassey and Field, under the supervision of Henry Robertson, the engineer. During 1860 plans were made and executed for altering the station and the siding layout at Craven Arms to accommodate the Knighton Railway and in March 1861 the line was opened to Knighton and by the late 1860s had linked with the line (the Central Wales Railway, which was how the whole line became known) coming up from the south-west to provide a route through to Llanelli, Swansea and beyond.

In these years two other railways had come to Craven Arms. The progress of the first of these, the Bishop's Castle Railway, had not been smooth, nor was it ever to be. On 28 June 1861 the Act "for making Railways from the Oswestry and Newtown Railway near Montgomery to Bishop's Castle and other places in the County of Shropshire" received Royal Assent. But there were grave difficulties with landowners on the western end of the line and with raising the necessary finance, while the contractor, Mr. Thomas Savin, was himself financially overstretched (in February 1866 the 'millionaire' Savin was reported to be craving "the temporary indulgence of his creditors") and had to

Bishop's Castle Railway mixed train at Craven Arms in the 1930s

be replaced. As a consequence work from 1864 onwards was concentrated on opening only the section of the line from Stretford Bridge, the proposed junction with the Shrewsbury and Hereford Railway just north of Craven Arms, and Lydham Heath, together with the branch line from there to Bishop's Castle. This part of the railway was opened on 24 October 1865, but by then only Plowden had any station buildings and it was not until 1 February 1866 that the first passenger service from Bishop's Castle to Craven Arms began. Within a year the Company was on the verge of bankruptcy. In December 1866 there were bailiffs at each terminus on the line, and one accompanying every train, though these ran as usual. On 23 January 1867 the Company's rolling stock was sold off, but the main purchaser, the Midland Wagon Company, decided to keep the line open and to carry on the existing service with its present staff.

The second railway came in from the east. In the early 1860s the Great Western Railway was developing a network of lines in the east of the County, from Wellington to Coalbrookdale and Much Wenlock. In 1860 a Company, called the Much Wenlock, Craven Arms and Coalbrookdale Railway, was formed and the Wenlock Railway Act was passed in July 1861. The line from Wenlock, one of whose purposes was to carry stone from the limestone quarries on Wenlock Edge, was opened to Presthope in December 1864 and reached its junction with the Shrewsbury and Hereford at Marsh Farm, 3 miles north of Craven Arms, three years later.

This completed the development of Craven Arms as a railway junction, but it did not end the genesis of schemes to build further railway lines past the Craven Arms Inn. Indeed, the lines already constructed were only those which had emerged successfully from a variety of proposals for routes which would have come this way. As early as 1836 when routes were being surveyed to open up communications from southern England with the ports which linked North Wales to Ireland, one line suggested from Porth Dynlleyn, the then proposed Packet Station on the Lleyn Peninsula, was to make its way southeastward out of Wales to Newtown and then by Snead (which is specifically named on the surviving map), Bishop's Castle, the Onny Valley to Ludlow, Tenbury Wells, Worcester and Oxford.

In 1845 plans were deposited for the Shropshire Mineral Railway to run from near Stafford through Newport, Madeley, Much Wenlock, Acton Round, Shipton and Diddlebury to terminate at Newton. Its prospectus described it as "forming, in conjunction with other existing and projected lines, a direct communication between Liverpool, Manchester, Sheffield, York and Hull and Swansea and South Wales." Among the provisional Committee were Thomas Beddoes of Cheney Longville, Francis Marston of Aston, Hopesay, William Plowden of Plowden Hall and Thomas Weyman of Purslow Hall, Clunbury.

In the Parliamentary Session of 1860-61 a South Staffordshire and Central Wales Railway was proposed. This was to come from near Dudley, making a junction with the Severn Valley Railway at Bridgnorth, and then on into and down the Corvedale, with a branch to Wenlock east of Shipton, and passing Culmington and Stanton Lacy, was to join the Shrewsbury and Hereford Railway at Ludlow Racecourse. A branch went on due west to join the Shrewsbury and Hereford and Knighton Railways at Craven Arms.

None of these schemes reached the statute book. But a later one with similar objectives did. This was incorporated in the Midland and Central Wales Junction Railway Act 1883. The purpose was still to "facilitate communication between the Midland Counties of England and Milford Haven and Swansea respectively." It would have taken a similar line to that proposed for the South Staffordshire Railway, connecting Craven Arms to Willenhall near Wolverhampton, and linking with both the Central Wales Railway and the Bishop's Castle Railway. As with its predecessors, despite Parliament's approval, no turf was turned, a fate similar to that experienced by the Presteigne, Clun and Bishop's Castle Railway, sanctioned by an Act of 1866, which would also have come by Craven Arms (as well as running from Hopton Heath, through Purslow and Clunton to Clun). The latter may have foundered because of the financial crisis in 1866, caused by the collapse of the finance company, Overend and Gurney, which had lent imprudently to railway projects. The former may have died because the hopes of establishing Milford Haven as a major port for the Atlantic trade did not bear fruit.

So Craven Arms did not become the 'Crewe of the West', as some have thought it was planned to be. But by the late 1860s the station and its associated yards were a bustling railway centre. By now, Thomas Brassey's original lease of the Shrewsbury and Hereford Railway having lapsed, the line was jointly leased by the London and North Western Railway, which also ran the Central Wales and Knighton Railways, and the Great Western Railway, which also ran the Wenlock Railway. Plans to double the line from Shrewsbury to Hereford, which had been the intention from the beginning, came under serious consideration in March 1859 and the Board of Trade sanctioned the opening of the double line to Ludlow in August 1862, the whole project through to Hereford being completed in 1863. A timetable of August 1870 shows nine passenger trains a day each way on the Shrewsbury to Hereford line, four trains out and five in on the Central Wales line, and three each way on both the Wenlock and Bishop's Castle lines.

The additional lines into Craven Arms Station and its position as a terminus required more facilities for passengers, goods, rolling stock and engines. In 1868 a larger shed for engines was planned and in 1871 a new carriage siding was provided. And traffic through the station continued to increase over the ensuing years, despite a hiatus of five months in 1877 while the Bishop's Castle Railway was closed as it sought to raise sufficient funds to satisfy one of its creditors. Developments of the railway system in South Wales in the 1870s led to an increase in the coal traffic coming from there to the industrial north-west, and the opening of the Severn Tunnel in 1886, together with gauge changes on the G. W. R., brought express traffic in both directions (from the south-west to the north and to Scotland) through Craven Arms. The Central Wales trains also carried through coaches between Swansea, Manchester and Liverpool.

This business needed staff to deal with

The engine sheds at Craven Arms Station

it. A station – designated after 1879 as Craven Arms and Stokesay – which had opened with a station master, a porter and a goods porter now required booking clerks, refreshment room staff, more passenger and goods porters, warehousemen, signalmen, a crossing keeper, carriage and engine cleaners, firemen and engine drivers. They had to be housed, in increasing numbers.

This, as well as the parlous state of the Bishop's Castle Railway, is brought out in the Petition to the House of Commons of John Jones of Grove against the Bishop's Castle branch of the Midland and Central Wales Railway in 1883. Remarking that he "has recently completed for his own occupation a residence with suitable gardens, stable, farm and other buildings,

The carriage sheds at Craven Arms Station

known as Grove, Craven Arms, at a cost exceeding £35,000, the site for this residence [having been] selected so as to provide extensive views over the adjacent junction of the Onny and Quenny Rivers" he contended that the branch to join the Bishop's Castle line was "absolutely useless", there being "no necessity for such connection, either as regards present or possible future traffic requirements....The traffic of all kinds on the Bishop's Castle line is trifling in quantity....there is no prospect of any increase, and the service of trains is scanty and irregular...The Bishop's Castle Railway Company are in such embarrassed circumstances that they are not in a position to conduct what traffic there is." "Some of the lands proposed to be taken [for the branch line]," he continued, "are valuable not only for agricultural purposes, but as having a large and ever-increasing element of value as building land. The existence of the present station at Craven Arms Junction has created a demand for building land in the neighbourhood, and large prices can easily be obtained for suitable sites."

The development of the town of Craven Arms was under way.

The Ordnance Survey Plan of 1903 (right) shows how the railway and auction yards dominated the development of Craven Arms

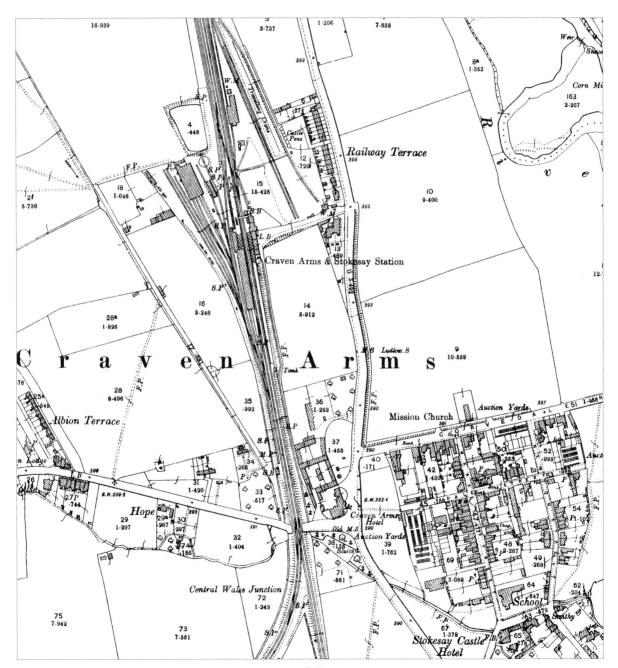

4: THE DEVELOPMENT OF CRAVEN ARMS

The line which the railway took through the Parish of Stokesay was almost exclusively on Craven land. The one exception was a field belonging to George Oldnall which broke into the sequence of Craven owned fields on the Shrewsbury road to the north of the Craven Arms Inn (see plan on page 33). It was on this field that the station and station house were built, the station approach and yard constructed, and the line of cottages for the first railway employees, which were to become Railway Terrace, began. Whether the choice of location, which is a quarter of a mile or so away from the road junctions and the hotel and over half a mile from Newton, was conditioned by the lie of the land and so by engineering considerations or by the fact that the Earl of Craven did not wish to give up more of his property than he absolutely had to cannot now be said. But, as will emerge, there is some evidence to suggest that it was the latter reason.

How much housing was originally provided for staff and the precise sequence of the development of Railway Terrace are not clear. By the late 1850s the Railway Board, responding to the success of the station, had decided to add to the number of cottages and in 1861 railwaymen and their families, including railway employee lodgers, occupied the eight dwellings which were there by then. The position was the same in 1871, but by 1891 there were seventeen numbered houses in Railway Terrace (in 1881 some were called Railway Cottages and some Railway Terrace). The large expansion was associated with the growth of the junction, but it was not confined to the vicinity of the station. For, about 1869 or 70 (they were described as the 'new cottages' in the 1871 Census), the London & North Western Railway began to build another row of railwaymen's housing on the site which became known as Newington Terrace, on the eastern side of the Shrewsbury road and rather more than a quarter of a mile to the north of the station. Why here? They were not especially conveniently located for railway workers. A possible answer is that they were not on Craven land (the Earl had been in a legal dispute with the L.&N.W.R. about access to the station in 1869). Indeed, they were not even in Stokesay but in Halford, on land

Newington Terrace

belonging to the Plymouth Estate – the Honourable R. H. Clive was one of the early Directors of the Shrewsbury and Hereford Railway. In 1871 eleven of the houses were taken (they were erected in two tranches of thirteen and fourteen) and by 1881 all twenty seven were occupied.

In 1861 there were 31 men employed on the railway living in the Parish of Stokesay. The most significant group of them were labourers and platelayers (13), mainly lodgers in Stoke and Park Lane, who, no doubt, were still working on the construction of the Knighton Railway. The Shrewsbury and Hereford Railway men lived in Railway Terrace or lodged in Newton. Many of the labourers were local, but the employees of the Railway Company came generally from further afield. There were clerks from Dublin, London and Hereford, a pointsman and a warehouseman from Scotland, a guard from Mold and an engine driver from Chester. This man, George Nicholls, stayed in Craven Arms for the next thirty years, moving into Newington Terrace when the new houses there opened in 1871. But he was an exception, since only one other railway family of the original group in Railway Terrace in 1861 was still there ten years later. It is clear both from the Railway Board minutes and from the census that the Railway Company men moved frequently, especially in these early years. For example, the guard from Mold, Thomas Griffiths, who was thirty, had four children, of whom the eldest had been born at Pontesbury where his wife came from, the second, aged 6, at Leominster and two, aged 5 and 2, at Shrewsbury. There was a sequence of Station Masters who followed the unfortunate Mr Walker, but Thomas Price was here for some years from 1856 onwards, during which time he added three children to his family, in 1856, 1857 and 1861 (his first child had been born at Abbey Foregate in Shrewsbury). Many of the early staff were young and either only just married or unmarried. Marriages between railwaymen and local women also begin to appear in the Stokesay Marriage Register, the first in 1860 being between William Pearce, a porter, and Mary Morris of Newton (however, Pearce was from Onibury, so this may have been a local romance).

By 1871 the majority of the unskilled labourers had gone and the railway staff (35 in all) were almost exclusively employed on 'professional' railway duties, most of them living in Railway Terrace or the newly built Newington Terrace – there were now no railway servants in Newton. Three signalmen had been added to the staff, a passenger guard, three firemen, another driver and the lady superintendent of the Craven Arms Station Refreshment Rooms (first licensed in 1870). The staff were still predominantly not local people – there was an engine cleaner from Tavistock and a fireman from Yorkshire – but a significant number of them now came from places close to or on the railway, Church Stretton, Ludlow, Leominster, Orleton and Shrewsbury, and one, Thomas Cadwallader, a porter, came from Whettleton. So the railway was, at last, starting to provide employment opportunity for local people other than simply as labourers.

The next 20 years saw the really substantial growth in railway staff living and working here or from here, from 35 in 1871, to 62 in 1881 and 84 in 1891. Railwaymen and their families made up about 15% of the combined population of Stokesay and Halford in 1871. By 1891 this proportion had increased to 25%, but, if only the parts of the parishes which became Craven Arms are considered, 44% (300) of its population of 684 were in 'railway' families..

In 1881 there were 5 drivers, 6 firemen and 5 guards (one of these, Albert Torr, from Slapton in Devonshire, was to play a significant part in the life of the town). Supervisory grades were coming more into evidence – a Railway Auditor, from Bruerne in Northamptonshire, a brakeman examiner, and a wagon inspector. There were two telegraph clerks and the bookstall had its own clerk also. And by this time some local men were getting specialist railway jobs – Charles Cadwallader, brother of Thomas, from Whettleton, an engine driver, Richard Biggs from Park Lane, Stokesay, a guard, William Cadwallader from Culmington, a fireman, Edwin Fewtrell, an engine driver from Munslow and Edward Lloyd, railway yard foreman from Clungunford. And railway staff were beginning to live with their families in properties other than Railway Terrace and Newington Terrace.

This trend continued through the 1880s. In 1891, although the great majority of railway staff still lived in Railway Terrace and Newington Terrace, nine railway families were established in other parts of Craven Arms and Newton. Furthermore, over a half of the families in Newington Terrace and a third of those in Railway Terrace had been there for ten years or longer. In Railway Terrace all the children of William Foster, at Number 1, of William Owen, at Number 3, of John Inskip at Number 4 and of Thomas Cadwallader at Number 6 had been born in Stokesay, while the children of 11 families in Newington had been born either all in Halford or some in Stokesay (at Railway Terrace) and some in Halford; and Foster and Inskip each had children who were employed on the railway. This signalled the increasing integration of the railway into the local community and, at the same time, the need for services of various kinds to be locally available for the railway, its staff and their families. This must have become noticeable from the mid-1870s onwards, as the railways settled down, the junction became established as a significant centre of railway business, and the staff began its substantial period of growth. But, apart from the original staff housing, the Railway Companies played no direct part in the development of the town, as had happened at places such as Crewe and Swindon.

Until the late 1870s the only new development in the area, other than the railway housing, was the Temperance Hall, later to be known as the Temperance Hotel. The Shrewsbury Chronicle of Friday, 12 May 1865 reported: "On Friday last the first stone of a building to be named the Craven Arms Temperance Coffee House and Reading Room" and situated close to the station of that name, on the Shrewsbury and Hereford line, was laid by Miss E. E. Lumb. The 46th Psalm was read by the Rev. W. E. Lumb, incumbent of Halford, on the occasion. Prayer was then offered by the Rev. T. P. Wilson, Rector of Smethcote; two suitable hymns were sung at the commencement and close of the ceremony. A meeting was afterwards held in a tent erected on the ground, when the Rev. T. P. Wilson delivered an address and a few words were spoken by the Rev. C. E. L. Wightman and Mrs Wightman. A 99 years' lease of the land has been kindly given by the Earl of Craven at a nominal rent. The funds for the erection of the building etc. are at present upwards of £200 short of the requisite amount, and further contribution will be very acceptable."

The temperance movement began in this country in the 1830s and by the 1850s there were two national bodies, the National Temperance League and the British Temperance League, but its strength lay in its local societies and their leaders. One of these, present and participating on this auspicious occasion, was Mrs Julia Wightman, the wife of the Vicar of St. Alkmunds in Shrewsbury. She was a vigorous campaigner for the movement in Shrewsbury and the surrounding district throughout her life, and her biographer reported that in 1865 "Of the 330 adults who signed the pledge this year many resided outside Shrewsbury. She had the satisfaction of inaugurating a new branch of her Society at Dorrington; and a temperance hotel, which was in reality a result of her work and influence, was opened in Craven Arms."

In this enterprise she had the considerable support of Mrs Emily Lumb, the wife of the Reverend William Lumb, vicar of Halford from 1842 to 1885. In 1875 Mrs Lumb published 'A Selection of Temperance Songs and Hymns', intended for the use of the Halford Temperance Society. This little book was made available to all lodgers at the Temperance Hotel. In her Preface Mrs Lumb observed "The compiler of the following Songs and Hymns has been led to their publication from the fact of her not having hitherto met with any similar collection, which does not contain some songs which might be

The Temperance Hotel

considered objectionable: it is hoped that this Selection will be found useful to abstainers for singing at their meetings and instructive also for non-abstainers, who may not have given the unspeakably important subject of Total Abstinence the attention it claims from all." In the early 1870s the Stokesay School Log Book has several references to the Temperance Hall. There were Temperance Tea meetings there in 1870, '71 and '72, which took children away from the school, and in March 1875 the "Band of Hope Children met at the Temperance Hall". Perhaps the latter meeting opened with the following song from Mrs Lumb's compilation: "A Band of Hope I love to see,/ Their singing's sweet to hear,/ Whose little hearts are filled with glee/ Without the aid of beer."

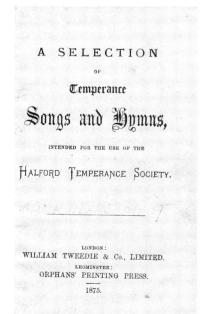

The first recorded keeper of the Hall, which was in the hands of The Craven Arms Temperance Reading Room and Coffee House Trust, was James Need, succeeded by 1871 by James Thomas Read. By that year it was described as the Temperance Hotel, and among its occupants when the census was taken were a commercial traveller with his wife and son, a farmer and two cattle drivers. Later in that decade Thomas Edge, a former railway servant, took over, and it was to remain under the proprietorship of his family down to the Second World War, when it was commandeered by the Army. In 1885 it is described as "a commercial and family temperance hotel, adjoining Railway Station; good accommodation for commercial gentlemen, every comfort for tourists, good fishing, horses and traps for hire, terms moderate."

For nearly thirty years from 1851 until the end of the 1870s the census and the trade directories indicate that such trades people, besides the inn- and hotel-keepers, as there were – a grocer, a 'shopkeeper', a shoemaker, the post master/mistress – were in Newton. The community's spiritual and educational needs were met near Stokesay Castle – the Vicarage had been built in 1839 just over the river from the church, and the school, opened in 1858, was close by (the plans for a capacity of 110 approved in 1857 show that the school authorities had by then realised that they would need something rather larger than the single room for 64 children originally designed in 1851). But in those thirty years the joint population of Stokesay and Halford had grown from 673 to 991, increasing further to 1225 in 1891. This increase was concentrated upon the area of the parishes which was by the mid-1880s called Craven Arms.

It is obvious from what happened on the ground from 1879 onwards that someone had recognised that Craven Arms must begin to grow into something more than just a settlement for railwaymen and their families. But who that was and what exactly were the causes of the decision and the sequence of events it is difficult now certainly to say. However an account can be constructed with some degree of confidence from a variety of sources. Probert's map of the Wolley estate in Stokesay of 1765, Baker's map of the Craven estate in Stokesay of 1772, the 1840s tithe map and the 1903 Ordnance Survey map of the town, which was based on a survey of 1883, enable an accurate picture to be assembled of land ownership when the period of development began. A number of key property conveyances from around the town for this period and later, a map for the sale of building plots in Craven Arms in 1881, together with the Parliamentary electoral rolls and the return of property ownership in 1912 made under the provisions of the Finance Act 1910, reveal contemporary property development and changes of ownership, and this information can be enhanced and fleshed out by the census, the dates and initials on various of the houses in the town, and the Directories of the time.

This part of the story begins with the establishment late in 1874 of the firm of Rogers and Hamar, auctioneers and valuers, the predecessors of Jackson and McCartney. With an office originally at Central House, Bucknell where they started to sell cattle in March 1875, they had recognised the potential of Craven Arms as an auction market, in view of the very substantial numbers of cattle and sheep which had been passing through the railway stock yards since the late 1850s. In April 1875 their first advertisement for an auction of fat and store cattle and of sheep – "to be held at Craven Arms at one o'clock on 3 May" – appeared in the Shrewsbury Chronicle. On Friday 28 May the newspaper announced that Messrs Rogers and Hamar would be holding an auction at Craven Arms on the first Monday in every month punctually at eleven o'clock throughout the year. For this sale "the entries include some very ripe Fat Wethers from Walcot Park and the surrounding neighbourhood – very choice Fat Lambs, prime Fat Cows and Oxen, Calves, Horses, Pigs etc.", and the next advertisement said that "they have been favoured with instructions from Mr F. Bach, Onibury to sell by auction at their second monthly sale on Monday 7 June at Craven Arms the Pedigree Bull, Clement, calved 10 May 1870 by Matchless, dam Clementine by Chieftain…" This was the beginning of the sheep and cattle market at Craven Arms.

But the firm did not content themselves simply with monthly sales. The great late summer sheep sales also started in 1875 and were to last for over a hundred years. In the Shrewsbury Chronicle of the 27 August, under the heading 'Important to Breeders of Shropshire Sheep', Messrs Rogers and Hamar begged "to announce that their first great sale of Pure Bred Shropshire Rams and Stock Ewes will be held in the Close adjoining the Craven Arms Railway Station and the Hotel on Monday next, 30 August, at 11.30 a.m. punctually. This important sale will comprise sixty Grand Shropshire RAMS and 600 Shropshire EWES of the purest lineage, from the well-known prize-taking flocks of Messrs Amies of Stoke; Bach of Onibury; Bach, Norton; Blakeway, Shelderton; Evans, Aston; Farmer, Felton; Rocke, Clungunford; and other distinguished breeders, and will afford a most desirable opportunity to purchasers of FIRST CLASS SHEEP for Breeding purposes. Craven Arms", it continued, "is situated in the centre of a very large neighbourhood which is justly celebrated for its innumerable beautiful specimens of the purely descended Shropshire Down, whose harmony of shape, abundance of flesh, excellence of quality, both of mutton and wool, and

the attribute to attain early maturity have raised this breed to the highest point of merit and caused it to be sought with the keenest avidity by practical farmers and eminent amateurs throughout the world." In December of that year they also inaugurated a great annual prize sale and show (cups of sterling silver were awarded) of pedigree bulls, cows, heifers and sheep for Christmas beef and mutton.

By 1879 Rogers and Hamar had acquired a portion of the area between what is now Corvedale Road and School Road – the former Grange Farm. This they had bought from the Oldnall family, in whose possession it had been certainly since the 1840s and probably from before 1765, since the Oldnall family and the Wolley family (the owners in the latter year) were undoubtedly related, the key player in the eventual disposal of their Stokesay estate being called Edward Clive Oldnall Long Phillips-Wolley (recorders of the time were somewhat uncertain, scarcely surprisingly, whether he was Wolley-Phillips or Phillips-Wolley). During the 1880s his address was given as Morgan Hall, Gloucester (1883) and School House, Highgate, London (1886), but by 1892, he had an address in British Colombia. Although the history of

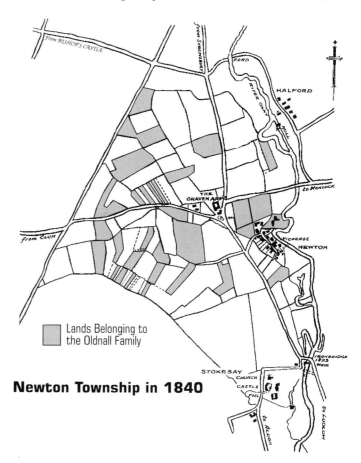

Lands Belonging to the Oldnall Family

Newton Township in 1840

ownership from earlier times cannot on present evidence be established, it seems likely that the Wolley-Oldnall estate was the land which before the dissolution of the monasteries had belonged to Haughmond Abbey.

It looks as if Phillips-Wolley, who had come into possession of the Oldnall properties in or about 1877 (Catherine Oldnall was the designated owner in 1876 and she died on 11 May 1877), perceived the value for development purposes of the land which he held hereabouts and decided to dispose of the estate. This happened over a period of some years. A plan dated about 1876 but of otherwise unknown context showed some of the property in the area of what is now Market Street as already sold to Rogers and Hamar. On the western side of this they established the Smithfield, their auction yard. In January 1879 an advertisement in the Shrewsbury Chronicle drew the attention of "builders, speculators and others" to the availability of valuable freehold building sites in Craven Arms. "Messrs. Rogers and Hamar will offer for sale at the Craven Arms Hotel by auction on Friday 7 February 1879 several highly desirable freehold building sites for private dwellings, business premises or offices." And early in 1882 it was announced that "Messrs Rogers and Hamar will sell by auction on Tuesday February 25th 1882 at 3 o'clock in the afternoon several valuable building sites leading from the Corvedale Road to the village of Newton."

A plan in the Record Office at Shrewsbury, signed James Bann, March 1881, but with no other identification, and entitled 'Plan of an Estate and Building Sites at Newton, Craven Arms', may relate to this sale. It designated Market Street as 'New Road' and Dale Street and Newton Street as 'Proposed Roads'. It showed four properties already built on Corvedale Road and two down the New Road (Market Street) – this would have been as a result of the 1879 sale. Most of the property on either side of Market Street was already disposed of; the rest of the land, roughly the area of Dale Street, Newton Street and the eastern end of Corvedale Road, was divided into 38 building lots.

The properties already in existence were: first, what is now the Spar shop, which was owned by Gaius Smith (Grocers) of Ludlow and in the 1881 census was called the General Stores and was occupied by David Smith, a butcher, who had, as his two lodgers, a grocer and a grocer's assistant; secondly, the building, now a private house next to the old Lloyds Bank building, which was marked Post Office on the plan, and has on it the date 1879 and the initials T. G. – Thomas Groves, the postmaster at that date (the conveyance of this land, called part of the Barn Yard, from Rogers and Hamar to Thomas Groves is dated 24 April 1879); thirdly the building, now Machin's furniture shop, which in 1881 was occupied by Francis Smith, a baker, whose servant was also a baker; and fourthly, the building on the east corner of Market Street, now Cyril Bason's, the ironmongers, which is marked Hotel on the plan, and has on it the date 1879 and the initials J.T.R., James Thomas Read, previously at the Temperance Hotel, who had now established another commercial hotel here, run by his wife Martha in 1881. Down Market Street, the two buildings shown on the 1881 plan are the Chapel, which is now the Catholic Church (this, the Primitive Methodist Chapel, had been opened on 29 June 1880, the land having been purchased in 1879 from Rogers and Hamar), and Rose Cottages at the bottom of the street, four cottages carrying the initials T.J., probably Thomas Jones of Newton, and dated 1881 – these can only just have been completed when the plan was drawn.

Building and the sale of land for building were proceeding apace. A few conveyances and building dates around the town give the picture. In Corvedale Road the conveyance for the land on which what is now The Paper Shop was built at the corner of Market Street dates from 1880 and a brick in the house bears the date 2 August 1883. The conveyance for Wilton House – Walls, the butchers – was in June 1882, from Phillips-Wolley to John Owens. Dale Villas, next door, bear the date 1882. In Market Street the four shops on the west side at the top bear the date 1880 and the initials G. E. – George Edge.

The Market Hall, according to Kelly's Directory, was built in 1889, a market being held every Friday. (But there is a record in the minutes of the Primitive Methodist Church to their holding a Christmas Tea Meeting in the Market

The construction of Craven Arms Market Hall c.1888

Hall on 25 December 1888; the minutes also refer to a concert in the New Assembly Room in the Market Hall in March 1889). The building next door to it, now called Market House, bears the date 1879, although it did not appear on the 1881 plan. Further down, on the east side below Dale Street, Clifton House is dated 1884 and at the bottom on the right Osborne House bears the initials T. J. and the date 1883. Also displayed are the tools of Thomas Jones' trade. He was the blacksmith, who had moved here from the smithy round the corner in Newton. The sequence of villas on the north side of Dale Street has dates of 1884 and 1893. In Newton Street the electoral roll of 1885 gave Edward Jones as the owner of Yew Tree Cottage and that of 1890 showed Prospect Place as occupied. But the terrace of houses opposite are dated 1906. Lower down Newton Street the Laurels bears the date 1894 and the initials T. D. – Thomas Davies. Davies, an engine driver then living at 20 Newington Terrace, had bought the plot from Edward Hotchkiss in 1893 (Edward Hotchkiss of Aldon had, in his turn, acquired it from Phillips-Wolley in 1886).

The Hotchkiss family were also involved elsewhere in the town's development out of the Oldnall estate. In addition to the fields immediately adjacent to the Grange Farm upon which central Craven Arms was built, Probert's Map of 1765 shows Thomas Wolley in possession of a number of fields or parts of fields to the west of the Shrewsbury road and George Oldnall had them in 1840. These were scattered among Craven owned land, and in some cases were strips within what had been the old open field system of Newton, notably four strips out of eight in a field called variously Little Woosthidge, Worsthedge, or Worsted on the northern side of the Clun road. On 24 March 1883 Henry Hotchkiss, then of Larden Grange, Much Wenlock, but connected with the Hotchkiss family of Aldon, bought from Phillips-Wolley 54 acres of the Oldnall estate, mainly in this western part of the town. Before 1891 he had built a house, Woodville, on the higher ground on the right above the Clun road, where he lived until his death in 1927; he is still remembered by some people. Parts of this land were then sold for housing.

In 1885 Dr Ernest Tredinnick, the town's first resident doctor, built a house, Penlu, at the western end of Lower Woosthidge field. Around 1890 Albion Terrace was built on another of the strips, which accounts for the narrowness of the plot and the angle which these cottages make with the Clun road. The person who developed this site seems to have been Thomas Lambe, who also built Wilton Lodge, the next property up the Clun road from Albion Terrace, where he was living in 1900. At the same time as Albion Terrace was being built another terrace (Milwaukee Terrace) was erected on the opposite side of the road in the Oldnall field called Road Meadow, and in 1905 Thomas Lambe (his initials are on the house) added Bryn-a-Wel onto the eastern end of the terrace. Coton House, the detached house at the top of the Terrace is dated 1892. Its deeds show that Charles Dayus, the veterinary surgeon, bought it in March 1904 from

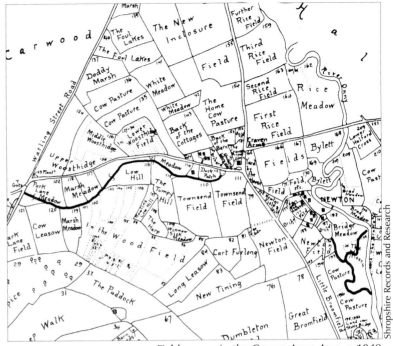

Field names in the Craven Arms Area, c.1840

Penlu House, Clun Road, from an old postcard

Thomas Lambe.

In the early 1960s Frank Noble, a notable local historian, ran a series of W.E.A. classes on the history of Craven Arms, one of the products of which was an article by him published in the Shropshire Magazine of February 1963. In this he wrote of Albion Terrace "In the 1880s a narrow strip in Woosthidge Field, with Craven strips on either side, was bought by a Mr Lamb who had recently returned from North America. He built Albion Terrace on it....Milwaukee Terrace may also be a record of Mr Lamb." Now it is just possible that there were two men called Lamb (one spelt with and the other spelt without the 'e') associated with development in this area of the town, but that seems a strange coincidence and there are other facts which tell against it.

Thomas Lambe of Wilton Lodge was undoubtedly the Thomas Lambe, who, for close on fifty years since the death of his father, also Thomas Lambe, in 1850, was the blacksmith at Newington. The Directories, the census and the electoral roll show him there continuously during this period, living latterly at Newington Villa. In 1891 he was described as a farmer rather than as a blacksmith; his wife, Jane, and an uncle, Richard Pugh, a retired farmer, lived with him. Richard Pugh's will, made in June 1891, left in the first instance to his nephew, Thomas Lambe, his (then) five houses of Milwaukee Terrace, which were described as "newly erected messuages". The 1896 electoral roll gives Richard Pugh as the owner of "6 houses, Milwankie [*sic*] Terrace" and in 1900, when Thomas Lambe had come to live at Wilton Lodge, Richard Pugh was there with him. Pugh died in 1902 and Lambe in 1908, and they are both buried at Halford and lie together with their Lambe relatives. On Thomas Lambe's death the Albion Terrace properties were left to the Barnes family, Mrs Barnes being a niece of Thomas Lambe, the Milwaukee Terrace houses having gone to various of Richard Pugh's nieces. It may have been Richard Pugh who had the American connection, returning at the end of his life to rejoin his family – he was born at Cheney Longville in 1810. Otherwise the origin of Frank Noble's account must, for the present, be a mystery. Whatever the answer to that is, it is clear that these two sites were developed by Thomas Lambe of Newington and his relative by marriage, Richard Pugh.

So much for the early domestic development of Craven Arms. Alongside it there was an increasing provision of supporting services. In 1877 the Craven Arms Gas Company was launched. It purchased a piece of land from the Earl of Craven just to the west of the station and built on it at the cost of about £3,000 a gas works and a house for the works foreman, Mr John Morris. It was operational by the spring of 1879, but it was soon in difficulties and was never to be more than marginally successful throughout the forty years of its independent life. Its main market was to be the railway, as is clear from a letter written in January 1883: "This Company was encouraged to establish works at Craven Arms upon the understanding that the Railway consumption would be one and threequarters to two million square feet per annum at 5/- [25p.] per 1,000 feet. The Company thereupon erected Works adequate to supply this, with a small margin for such other consumption as could be obtained. While the works were in progress the Railway Company demanded that the gas should be supplied at 4/- [20p.] per 1,000 feet and under direct threat of not using it at all this had to be conceded. The total consumption for both the Joint Railway Company and the L. & N. W. R. has not reached one million feet in any one year and has therefore been only half the estimated amount, while the small consumption which can be obtained from other sources has not been sufficient to pay the interest on the cost of the mains and services." The Railway Company gave this letter short shrift, and when, later in the year, the Gas Company gave notice of a rise in the price of gas the Railway Company informed them that if they went ahead with it the railway would use no more gas. The notice was withdrawn.

The Company had, however, made every effort to extend the use of gas in the town and continued to do so. In 1880 a main was to be laid in "the New Street near Newton Village at an estimated cost of £15", and extended into the village itself. And in 1882 one was laid in Corvedale Road down to "Mr Owens' premises" – John Owens was the first owner of Wilton House (Wall's, the butchers) at the eastern end of the town. The

Company almost went bankrupt in 1887 but managed to soldier on through the goodwill of its debenture shareholders, even making profits in the 1890s of over £100, and being able for some years to pay 1% to the ordinary shareholders. It finally succumbed in 1918, selling out to the Ludlow Gas Company.

The provision of water and of a sewerage system for the developing town took some years to sort out. Under provisions of 1871 the responsibility for these systems fell upon the Sanitary Authority of the Ludlow Union – an extension of the duties of the Ludlow Poor Law Board of Guardians, as the local arm of the Local Government Board. A scheme devised in 1884 failed to make progress, even though the Sanitary Authority made preparations for the appointment of an engineer for the purpose in November of that year. In the early 1890s matters came to a head with concerns being expressed by the local Medical Officer of Health, Dr. Thursfield, about the possibility of an outbreak of cholera because of the quality of the water available and the quite inadequate means of disposing of sewage, some being put into cess pools, some into imperfect sewers, while some went into tanks which were pumped up and allowed to run into the stream. Severe illness had occurred and the smell and leakage from the tanks and cess pools caused periodic nuisance.

Revealing light is thrown upon Dr Thursfield's concerns by the deteriorating infant mortality rate in the Parishes of Stokesay and Halford as set out in the table above. The figures have been calculated from the burial and christening registers of those parishes in the hundred years from 1840 to 1939. The Halford figures are included not only because Newington Terrace stood in that Parish but also because in the middle years of the period a significant number of children from Stokesay Parish were christened there. Clearly the figures need to be treated with care since they record only christenings and burials which took place at the

INFANT MORTALITY IN THE PARISHES OF STOKESAY AND HALFORD 1840 -1939			
DECADE	NUMBER OF CHRISTENINGS	BURIALS OF CHILDREN UNDER ONE YEAR OLD	MORTALITY RATE PER THOUSAND CHRISTENINGS
1840 – 49	199	18	90
1850 – 59	225	26	115
1860 – 69	254	33	130
1870 – 79	305	34	111
1880 – 89	298	41	138
1890 – 99	217	47	217
1900 – 09	237	33	139
1910 – 19	213	17	80
1920 – 29	169	3	18
1930 – 39	171	7	41

two churches, and not necessarily all children, especially later in the period, were christened either at those churches or at all, nor were they necessarily buried there. By way of comparison, at Ludlow in 1899 where the Council had been dragging its feet over a new sewerage scheme and where some of the housing was very poor, the death of infants under one year stood at 183 per thousand births against an average over the previous twenty years of 143, while in the rural parishes of Norbury and Lydbury North the rate for the ten years from 1891 to 1900 was 70. In England and Wales as a whole the 1890s was the decade in which infant mortality reached its peak of about 150 deaths per thousand births.

Exploratory bore holes on Windsor Clive land close to the river east of the Shrewsbury road, near to where Norton View has now been built, showed that an adequate pumped supply of excellent domestic water was available from that source (Dr Thursfield describing it as "the best deep well water I have ever met with") and Lord Windsor was prepared to lease the land at a peppercorn rent. Despite some problems over the method of pumping water – by wind or oil driven pump – the water system was in place by 1894 – Dr Thursfield being instructed in November to test the well water in properties close to the mains, and if it was not satisfactory to cause them to be connected to the public main.

But J. D. Allcroft, since 1869 the owner of the Stokesay estate (the Earl of Craven still retained the Craven Arms Inn and its associated farmland in the northern part of the parish), was totally opposed to the establishment of a sewage works on his land – the site of choice was to the south of Stokesay Castle. He was a member of the Board of Guardians and therefore of the Sanitary Authority, but throughout the autumn and early winter of 1892 when the Authority were seeking to get the scheme off the ground he used every device to block and delay it – not attending meetings, rejecting the overtures of a deputation of his colleagues, claiming, when he did attend a meeting, that he had not been served with the plans, thus causing further delay, and then setting terms for leasing the land which were unacceptable to the Authority on grounds of cost. Finally, in December, the Authority was driven to seek powers of compulsory purchase – Allcroft did not attend the meeting at which the decision was taken, but gave written notice that he would object. At a public enquiry on Thursday 10 February 1893 Henry Hotchkiss, Edward Hotchkiss and Thomas Lambe "proved that the inhabitants of Craven Arms were strongly in favour of the scheme", but Allcroft remained opposed, on the grounds, as his representative said, that he owned two-thirds of the parish and the bulk of the rate would fall on him. However the matter was resolved during 1893 and during 1894 preparations were made for the sewage works to be built, with Herbert Allcroft, his father having died, agreeing to the terms for the lease of his land and a Clerk of Works being appointed in October. But the work took time to complete and, although a water rate began to be paid in May 1895, the Parish Council's minutes recorded that the Council, having requested the District Council in September 1895 to complete the water and sewage works as soon as possible, were constrained in March 1896 to appeal directly to the Local Government Board to intervene to put into proper condition the public water mains and sewers with which "the streets of Craven Arms were already laid".

The increase in the number of children in the community and the location of many of them in the northern part of the parish were by the early 1880s beginning to give problems to the Stokesay School Managers, even though, through the generosity of Lady Windsor Clive, a school for 60 children with a house for the school mistress had been built at Halford and opened in July 1876. This, no doubt took many of the youngest Newington Terrace children, but by 1885 numbers at Stokesay were sometimes running over 130 in a school which in the 1860s had rarely taken more than 80. A purpose-built school having comparatively recently (1858) been provided close to the church at Stokesay, which was of reasonably convenient access for the children from the southern end of the Parish, the Stokesay School Managers first response was to enlarge it. And this was done in the autumn of 1885, much to the inconvenience of the teachers and children – "The school is not nearly finished and many of the parents keep their children home being afraid of the damp." wrote the master on 16 October 1885. But the School Inspectors remained very critical of the accommodation, and the school was in other sorts of difficulty.

The school was a National School, that is to say it was a Church of England School established under the auspices of the National Society for Promoting the Education of the Poor in the Principles of the Established Church. As a voluntary school it relied for its income and its ability to pay the teachers' salaries upon such endowments as had been made in the past, subscriptions from local people, fees paid by parents (the so-called 'school pence') and government grants, which were paid upon the basis of attendance and performance at annual examinations conducted by the School Inspectors. To be viable the school needed supportive supervision by the School Managers and energetic, experienced and lively leadership and teaching from the master and his staff. Otherwise, to use the words of a study by T. D. M. Jones of the *"Development of Educational Provision in the Rural County of Salop between 1870 and 1914"*, a vicious circle developed of poor results, low grants, poor teachers, and poor attendance. "The recruitment and retention of an efficient staff and the maintenance of regular attendance in a county with so many small and isolated schools constituted two main preoccupations of those charged with the provision of educational facilities in Shropshire in the last quarter of the nineteenth century."

The Reverend James Digges La Touche, an Irishman – he had been ordained priest by the Lord Bishop of Cork, Cloyne and Ross in 1851 – had been vicar of Stokesay since 1855. He was an antiquarian and geologist of some note and, as its Manager, had been actively involved in the school from its earliest days. The log book recorded him as coming into the school virtually daily in the 1860s (this involvement declined a little over the years) to teach Latin, Euclid, Algebra, Geography, Shorthand and Chemistry. He instructed boys in turning on the lathe and took them out to learn land surveying. To begin with this won the approval of the School Inspector: "There is no school in my district in which the Manager takes so close an interest or in which the children have a better, I may say, so good an opportunity of gaining a good education, if only they stay long enough in the 1st Class" said the Inspection Report in 1867. But by the 1880s a different view was being taken, the Report of 1885, which was generally very critical, observing "Algebra and Euclid are well taught, but I think the teacher has hardly staff enough to justify the withdrawal of time from more elementary work". By 1887 the master reported that "The Reverend La Touche has given up Algebra this year with the upper children, in order that the master may have more time with them." It took a very determined master to achieve a balanced working relationship with a School Manager – effectively his employer – who was better educated, a well established and respected member of the community and a person by experience and position of far greater power than he was. What could be achieved by such a man may be seen at Clunbury where, the master from 1877 to 1919, William Deacon, ultimately succeeded in working most effectively in harness with the Reverend William Jellicorse to produce an excellent school.

Stokesay was not so fortunate and a succession of young and inexperienced masters (a number of whom were uncertificated on arrival) came and went. There were at least eight between 1863 and 1890, when Thomas Mountford, who was to stay until his retirement in 1925, took over (one, Edwin Stace, stayed for less than a year in 1873). Mountford was shocked by what he found: "Standards III, IV, V, VI, and VIII know very little at all. The discipline and tone of the school are disgraceful. The school fees have been utterly neglected and many of the children are in arrears." Mountford set about reforming the school (from 1891 onwards the vicar was reported as coming into the school only in his capacity as Manager), but by now it was too late to save it as a voluntary school run by the Church of England.

The Elementary Education Act of 1870 had made provision for rate-financed education to be provided, where there was no alternative, under the supervision of School Boards elected from the local community. Despite a brief flurry of activity in 1891, which included an appeal to the Railway Company to increase its subscription to the school, in October 1892 The Ludlow Advertiser reported that it had been found necessary to adopt measures for the election of a School Board. "The schools in Stokesay were formerly carried on by voluntary contribution but owing to the falling off of subscriptions and for the continuance of the school the above scheme has been decided upon. The Board will consist of five members." These were duly elected from a field of ten, and according to the school log book entry on 25 May 1893 "The management of Stokesay National School was transferred from the Manager to the Stokesay School Board".

But the problems with the building remained unresolved. In 1894 the Inspector, referring to the crowded and inconvenient premises, said: "There is urgent need of relief and, until this is afforded by new buildings, both Teachers and children will continue to suffer...Looking to the warning given last year that no further grants would be paid until new buildings were provided or the present ones brought strictly into accordance with the requirements of Article 85(a) of the Code, and that nothing has yet been done to remedy the defects in the buildings pointed out last year, payment of the grant has been suspended until My Lords are in receipt of information that the new buildings are well in progress."

That produced action. An option was taken on a site for the new school at the bottom of Market Street. The School Board were, however, compelled to defend this choice at a Public Meeting in November 1894. The site was criticised as damp, close to the stream and therefore unhealthy, and too far from the southern end of the parish, but the opposition came from people in the town rather than from the surrounding community. However the School Board did not own the existing school and were reluctant to invest money into

Stokesay School in Market Street

improving what was, in any case, an unsatisfactory building. They were advised that it would cost almost as much to alter it as to purchase the site for and build a new school (the figure quoted in the newspaper report was between £2,000 and £3,000). Having rejected sites offered by the Earl of Craven and Mr Allcroft at £700 and £600 respectively, and in face of the demands from the School Inspectorate for the children to be housed in premises which were adequate to their task, they were driven to override the objections (the Public Meeting voted overwhelmingly against the Market Street site), a contract was signed in the summer of 1895 and the new school opened on 31 August 1896. (Its transfer to the town may, perhaps, account for the disappearance from the pages of Kelly's Directory of the ladies' school which in 1891 was being run in Market Street by the Misses Augusta Robinson and Victoria Ashmore.)

Just as the school authorities had been forced to come to terms with the development of the town and the consequent shift of the balance of population in the parish, so too was the church. In its case there were other considerations. In 1871 J. D. Allcroft built a property in Newton – it bears that date and his initials – which was used as a Baptist Chapel, the minister being Matthew Matthews, who was a cooper by trade (there are stories of him preaching outside the Red Lion and conducting baptisms in the River Onny behind his house in Newton). There was already a Wesleyan Methodist Chapel at Longville, a little to the north of the parish, and, as already mentioned, a Primitive Methodist Chapel had been built in Market Street in 1880 (of the ten members of its eleven man General Purposes Committee in 1894 whose professions can be identified, six were railwaymen, two grocers, a tailor and a blacksmith). Sometime in the early 1890s the Plymouth Brethren established a meeting house in the town. This may originally have been in the building in Dale Street which is now the Pilgrim Centre (a baptismal chamber was found there when conversion work was being done). In 1907 it was described as a "building then or lately used a Mission Room", but by 1912 it was in a wooden hall at the north end of Newton Street. The Reverend La Touche felt that the Church of England had to become more closely involved with the town. Extracts from his correspondence at the time reveal what happened.

On 15 March 1894 he wrote to Herbert Allcroft: "You will, I dare say, remember that I spoke to you a short time ago about having a church built at Craven Arms. I am still of the opinion that if a sufficient sum can be raised, it ought to be a thoroughly good one, but if that cannot be it would be better to commence with a temporary building....I have every reason to hope that when Lord Craven's land comes onto the market, a site will be reserved for this purpose. In the meantime, I have...come to the conclusion that something might be done to prepare the way for the desirable object, but do not see my way to carry it out without your help. I therefore trouble you with this. The plan proposed is that a curate should be appointed to work among the people there." He then went on to say that he was prepared to meet half of the curate's salary from his own pocket and to ask Allcroft to meet the balance. "I have tried to do all I can to cope with the wants of the place" he continued, "but increasing years do not add to one's vigour while the number to be attended to and the difficulties of the work increase. So that a state of things is fast growing up which is far from desirable, and without help I cannot hope to do much to prevent it. I believe that if an energetic young man were appointed as curate, he might do a world of good. The population is torn asunder by dissent. I have no ill-feeling against conscientious dissent. But the form it takes here does not, I am convinced, contribute to the good of the people either morally or socially, and it might fairly be expected that the sober church system carried out in their midst would have a most beneficial influence."

Herbert Allcroft's reply of 17 March while praising the initiative and La Touche's self-sacrifice was not entirely helpful. "You ask me to be responsible for the balance. I think this is scarcely fair. Craven Arms has a far larger claim on Ld. Craven and Mr. Greene [owner of Grove Estate, Wistanstow], both richer men than myself, than it has on me. If they will give 10 guineas each I will give a like sum and Craven Arms ought to contribute the other 20....As you know Craven Arms has never treated either I [sic] or my father very well, and I don't see that the burden should fall on me as Ld. Craven owns the place and Mr Greene lives much closer than I do."

Despite the indignation of La Touche's friend, the Reverend William Jellicorse, the Vicar of Clunbury "I deeply sympathise with you in the disappointment you must feel by Allcroft's answer to you. He deserves to have his letter thrown in his face...What wretched cant." (from a letter of 4 April 1894) and an approach from the Bishop, Mr Allcroft held his ground. Lord Windsor, who was also approached, and Mr Greene were unforthcoming, but Lord Craven offered the lease of a site for a temporary church and at a well-attended public meeting at the Market Hall in August 1895 a resolution was unanimously passed "That this meeting, recognising the urgent need for additional church accommodation in this parish, in consequence of the increasing population of Craven Arms, heartily approves the proposed appointment of a curate, and pledges themselves to support it to the best of their power."

The Reverend La Touche, who chaired the meeting, was reported as saying in the course of his introduction: "They had in that community several places of worship carried on by Nonconformist friends; and he felt sure that everyone present would bear him out when he said from the first they had never had any friction or ill-feeling between them and the church. (Applause.) He was extremely proud that such should be the case, and as proof of that, in calling that meeting he saw several of his Nonconformist friends and they all met him in the most cordial manner, and he believed many of them were here this evening (Applause.)....His own opinion was – and many would agree with him – that they owed a great debt of gratitude to their Nonconformist brethren for their efforts to keep up a spirit of religion among the people. (Applause.)....He would be sorry to see the day when the Church should descend to the position of merely a sect competing with other sects. That being the case, he thought nobody could refuse them the privilege of endeavouring to do all the good they could in their own way; and he felt quite sure that they would receive cooperation, where it was desirable, from those among whom they lived. (Hear, hear.)" After the passing of the principal resolution the Bishop of Hereford, on his first visit to the town, spoke at some length and the meeting closed with a vote of thanks to the Bishop, seconded by Mr Matthews, the Baptist Minister, who "hailed the day when they would have a church at Craven Arms, and it was a pleasure to see unity among all Christians. (Applause.)"

Sufficient funds were forthcoming to enable a curate (Mr. Robertson Honey) to be appointed and, as is clear from an undated letter from the Reverend La Touche to the Church Friendly Society, soliciting their financial support, a Mission Church was erected. It stood on the north side of the Corvedale Road a little to the west of Mayfield Avenue. "Since the opening of the Mission Church in February 1896 there is good reason to believe that the advance of dissent has been decidedly checked. The services have been well attended. The church which holds 150 has frequently been quite full."

While Herbert Allcroft was willing to give some financial help towards meeting the spiritual needs of the people of Craven Arms, he was also not inattentive to their bodily requirements and of those engaged in the increasing trade coming to Craven Arms. The old inn in Newton was tucked away from the main road and too far from the market centre to give adequate support to the Craven Arms Hotel. The Return of Licensed Houses in 1896 reported that notice had been given that an application would be made at the next

An early postcard of Corvedale Road

licensing sessions for the licence of the Red Lion (William Street was the last licensee) to be transferred to "a house now in the course of erection near to these premises". This was The Stokesay Castle, opened in 1898 under the management of Richard Hartshorn and built on Allcroft land as close as could be achieved to the hub of activity in the newly created town. The Red Lion was eventually pulled down in the 1920s.

Over the fifty years since the coming of the railway the face of the northern part of the Parish of Stokesay had substantially changed. At the start of the period the pace of change was slow and made by single steps, but from 1875 onwards developments came pell mell, as the new settlement of Craven Arms came into being. In 1851 the population of Stokesay was 532 and of Halford 141; in 1871 689 and 198; in 1891 942 and 283 and in 1901 1006 and 257. In short, the population of the two parishes had increased by 88%, while the population of Shropshire as a whole was increasing by just under 5%; indeed the county's population actually declined slightly between 1871 and 1901. All of the increase was concentrated on the area associated with the station and its yards; the rest of the parishes' townships – Aldon, Rowton, Whettleton, the hamlet of Halford, and Dinchope

The Stokesay Castle Hotel

– continued in their rural way.

The 1856 edition of Kelly's Directory listed six tradesmen in Stokesay: a blacksmith, a wheelwright, a lime burner, a shoemaker, a shopkeeper and a milliner, all of them living in Newton, where the post office was also located (one delivery and one dispatch a day), together with the keepers of the two Inns and two coal merchants already at the station. Fifteen years later, in 1871, the picture was not very different; there were now three coal merchants and a timber merchant at the station, another hotel (The Temperance Hotel), and one more shop keeper (a

An early postcard of Newton. The Red Lion is on the right

butcher), but the milliner was no longer recorded. The Post Office arrangements remained the same.

By 1900 Craven Arms had, in addition to the Market Hall (the Secretary was Henry Hotchkiss who had taken over from George Rogers), about fifty shopkeepers, offering virtually every kind of service that people might require – grocers, butchers, fishmonger and poultry dealer, bakers and confectioners, wine and spirits merchant, boot and shoe shops, clothes and hat shops, ironmonger, chemists, seedsman, newsagents, book seller, photographer, hairdresser, fancy goods, watchmaker and china and glass dealer. There were a wheelwright, a blacksmith, a carpenter, a stone mason and a coal merchant. Professional services were offered by a solicitor, three bank branches, opening on Mondays and Fridays, an agent of the Prudential Insurance, a doctor, and a veterinary surgeon. There were two firms of auctioneers and valuers – Jackson and McCartney, who had taken over the original business of Rogers and Hamar (subsequently Rogers and Rogers) in 1893, on the Smithfield on the western side of town, and Morris, Marshall and Poole on the

An early postcard of Dale Street, looking west

Smithfield at the eastern end of Dale Street (this had been established by W. G. Preece, a Shrewsbury auctioneer in 1887). In addition to the three hotels there were five refreshment rooms, four in the town, the fifth being on the station. Postal services had increased to two deliveries and collections, morning and afternoon, each day, and a Sunday collection. Money orders were available at the Post Office on weekdays, as was a telegram service. The town had its own police constable since the 1880s; the police station was in Newton.

This was virtually the only service for the

community as a whole, apart from the Baptist Chapel, that was to be found in Newton itself. There was a butcher there and a grocer, Joseph A. Green, on the corner of School Road and Newton, but otherwise the shops were concentrated on Corvedale Road, Market Street and Dale Street. Although there were dwelling houses in these streets, the principal residential areas were Newton Street, Newton itself, which retained a small agricultural community, the railway houses, and the developments up the Clun Road, where some of the larger houses, like Penlu, Wilton Lodge and Coton House had been built.

Craven Arms was by the end of the nineteenth century a well developed, thriving and virtually self-sufficient community, with a range of public services, shops, trades and businesses which made it comparable in status (if not in population) to

An early postcard of Market Street, looking north. The Market Hall with its verandah may be seen on the right

other small market towns in the area – a status perhaps signalled when on 1 January 1898 The Ludlow Advertiser became The Ludlow Advertiser and Craven Arms Gazette. It had come to this condition over the last quarter of the century, following the establishment of the station as a junction. This had two key effects. The consequent growth in staff employed by the railway and their permanent settlement around the junction generated a need for them and their families to be provided with the necessaries of life and the other services which go with community living. And secondly, reinforcing that effect, the junction gave a trading focus for the surrounding area, a market which could use the transport facility offered by the railway to exploit more readily and effectively than ever before the commercial potential of stock raising in the region.

Jackson and McCartney's auction yard

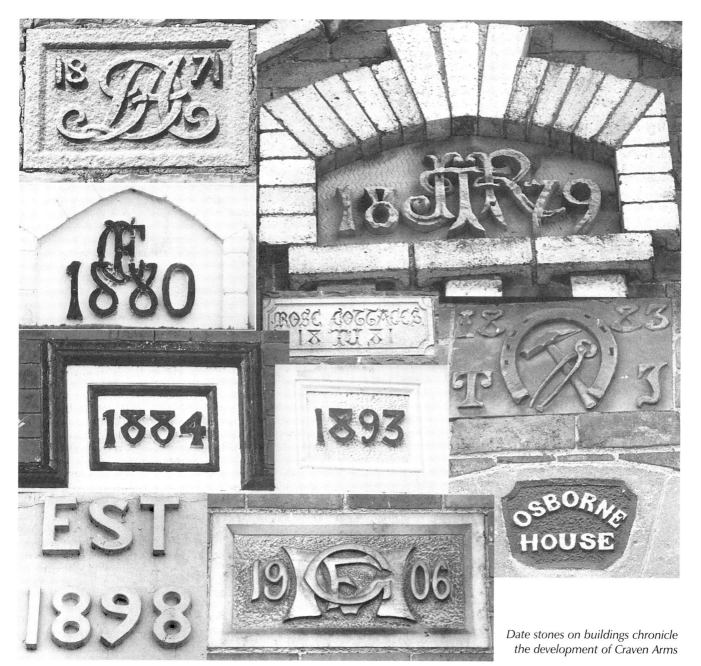

Date stones on buildings chronicle the development of Craven Arms

5: THE LIFE AND TIMES OF CRAVEN ARMS TO 1939

On Tuesday 4 December 1894 the ratepayers of Stokesay met at the Stokesay Board School to elect a Parish Council under the provisions of the Local Government Act 1894, which brought to an end the responsibilities of the Parish Vestry. Mr Rogers, a local businessman, took the chair. He told the meeting that they had the option to call for a poll, but "knowing how high the rates were at Craven Arms, he hoped that it would be their desire not to go to a poll – which would cause unnecessary expense". The only other reported speaker, before the meeting voted to select their council, was Mr Groom, of Stokesay Castle Farm. He hoped that they would agree to elect two agricultural members, namely Mr Meddins of Whettleton and himself. While the vote was being counted, the Reverend La Touche availed himself of the opportunity to speak. He said "he looked upon this movement with the greatest interest, and firmly believed that it was step in the right direction – that it would call to life the rural parishes like theirs. He heartily congratulated them on having a Parish Council. The first year perhaps might be a year of storm and he himself believed it might be one of hard work. Theirs was not an ordinary parish; they were no longer the homely quiet villagers of 40 years ago when he first came to the parish, but had a great influx of population coming in contact with the old. They must all give and take and he was sure that would be the motto of their members who were all good men and true."

When the votes were counted those elected to the Council were: Thomas Edge of the Temperance Hotel, George Farrell, railwayman of Milwaukee Terrace, Joseph Green, grocer of Newton, Herbert Groom, of Stokesay Castle Farm, Richard Hooper, railwayman of Railway Terrace, John Hough, railwayman of Dodds Lane, Matthew Matthews, Baptist Minister of Newton, Charles Salmon, draper of Corvedale Road, and Joseph Speed, railwayman of Newton Street. Of these men only four (Edge, Green, Groom and Matthews) had certainly lived here for more than eight years and only Edge and Matthews were recorded in the 1881 census. Four (Farrell, Hooper, Hough and Salmon) did not appear in the 1891 census.

When the make-up of this Council is compared with the people who had run the parish in the past the contrast is striking in three respects. The minutes of the Vestry Meeting from 1852 down to 1894 enable some picture to be drawn of the parish's senior members during that period. They were usually farmers, they were of long standing in the parish, and they came from all parts of it – Aldon, Whettleton, Weo, Rowton, Newton and Stoke. The overseers appointed in 1891 were Dervies Beddoes of Whettleton and Thomas Bromley of Step-Aside. When in 1851 the Vestry resolved to build a new school, the members appointed to the building committee were, in addition to the vicar, Mr Bache, Rowton, Mr Beddoes, Rowton, Mr Bishop, Aldon, Mr Marston, Weo, Mr Morris, Stoke Castle Farm, and Mr Sheppard, Whettleton. They were all farmers. The School Board elected in 1892 comprised Mr Green, a grocer, who hailed from Great Ness, Mr

G. Rogers, auctioneer, corn merchant and horse dealer, from Radnorshire, the Reverend La Touche, Mr H Groom, Stoke Castle Farm, who was from Wellington, Salop, and Mr. W. Hide, landlord of the Craven Arms Hotel, from Eaton under Haywood.

That change in the circumstances of those who held positions of responsibility in the parish in the 1890s is equally clearly brought out by a comparison of the origins of the heads of household who were living in Craven Arms and its immediate neighbourhood in 1891 and those in the same area in 1851. In that year 49% had been born in the parish of Stokesay itself, 18% within a radius of 7 miles from the parish, 21% further afield in Shropshire, and 12% were from outside the county; that is, two thirds were local people and a third were incomers. In 1891 the position was broadly reversed. 10% originated in Stokesay, 28% were from within 7 miles of the parish, 28% came from further afield in the county, and 34% were from outside Shropshire; that is a balance of 38% locals and 62% outsiders. The Reverend La Touche's remarks about the altered character of the community were well taken.

But his forecast that the first year of the Council's life would be stormy seems, from the evidence of the Council's minutes, to have been too pessimistic. Maybe it was his own accomplished chairmanship of the Council which smoothed the Council's path (he was co-opted chairman at the first meeting and was to remain so until his death early in 1899, being succeeded by an elected member of the Council, Thomas Edge – the practice from thenceforth). Maybe the elected members were indeed "good men and true" who adopted "the motto of give and take". But the more likely reason is that the Council represented, and has continued to represent, the interests of the newly developed community very precisely. Those focused upon Craven Arms. References in the Council's minutes to matters concerning the settlements away from the town occur very infrequently – the need for a post box at Aldon in 1899/1900 and again in the 1930s and for a telephone kiosk at Brand Hill in 1948 are instances. In general such difficulties and disputes as there were in the Council arose from conflicting interests within the town or between Stokesay and the Ludlow Rural District Council or the County Council rather than from disputes between the new-comer inhabitants of Craven Arms and the old-established residents of the rural neighbourhood.

An early and rare exception to this rule centred upon the lighting of the town. The issue, which was first raised in 1895, was whether the provisions of the Lighting and Watching Act 1833 should be adopted so that the cost of lighting the town could be charged upon the rates. Not surprisingly there was resistance to the notion that the whole parish should be rated for this purpose. The matter dragged on for almost fifteen years. Twice, in 1902 and 1904, a proposal for the adoption of the Act was put to a public meeting and twice it failed to pass, until ultimately in 1909 it was carried by 44 votes to 22. A rate was set of not more than 3d. [1.5p.] in the pound for the cost of erection of nineteen lamps and of not more than 1d. [0.4p.] in the pound for their lighting. The Craven Arms Gas Company provided the gas and the lights were lit by the lamp lighter (Mr George Corbett, appointed after a contested election in the Council), initially from 45 minutes after sunset until 10 p.m. In 1923 – electricity having come to the town – the Council agreed to convert to electric street lighting, subject now to the approval of the Rural District Council and the County Council.

Over the ensuing years most of the major issues that engaged the Council's attention were ones for which they did not have primary responsibility. Within ten years of the installation of the town's water supply complaints were being made to the Ludlow Rural District Council about the inadequacy of the system, although when, in 1910, the District Council proposed a gravitation system, Craven Arms rejected it as being too expensive and because the pumping system worked perfectly well. That did not deter the Council from dispatching two letters in November 1911, one to the Local Government Board to the following effect "Having regard to the shortness of the supply of water in this parish due to the inefficient state of the present pumping plant and the fact that the Local Water Committee as far back as March 1910 and a Parish Meeting convened on the recommendation of the Ludlow R.D.C. in November 1910 recommended the remodelling of the present pumping plant, the Local Government Board should make inquiry with a view to having the wishes of the ratepayers put into operation without further delay." The second, to the District Council, read "This Council are of the opinion that no further time should be wasted in considering imaginary water schemes but that the recommendations of the Local Committee of March 1910 and the Ratepayers' Meeting of November 25 1910 to remodel the present pumping system should be forthwith put into operation." It was to be a further ten years, which saw yet another Public Meeting, a Local Government enquiry, the examination and rejection of a scheme to bring water from Sibdon, and repeated representations to the District Council, before the Council made a final effort. A joint resolution from the Stokesay and Halford Councils was sent in February 1920 to the Minister of Health complaining about the District Council's failure to produce a good water supply; it noted that special pumping plant had been bought in September 1919 to improve the supply but it had failed to do so, and spoke forebodingly of the risk of epidemic through the inadequacy of water for washing and flushing. Thereafter complaints about the water supply disappear from the minutes of the Council.

In the fifty years from 1851 to 1901 the population of Stokesay Parish had almost doubled. After further growth from 1006 to 1142 in the first decade of the last century, it remained broadly steady for the next forty years (the 1951 figure was 1163). But decline in the population in the outlying settlements has been balanced by and so concealed growth in Craven Arms itself. Certainly from the mid-1920s onwards securing more housing at public expense in the town, which was a matter ultimately for the District Council, became, and was to remain, a preoccupation for the Parish Council. The great flush of house building in the 1880s and 1890s had been concentrated on land bought from the former Wolley-Oldnall estate in the centre of Craven Arms and along the Clun Road. That was virtually exhausted and the Craven Estate gradually began to release parts of its remaining estate.

Early steps were small. Two pieces of land were sold up the Shrewsbury Road towards Newington Terrace in 1906 and 1910 upon which houses called Blenheim and Clifton were erected, and about 1910 the Craven Estate built four new cottages at the bottom of the Clun Road by the railway bridge. There things remained until after the 1914-18 War, when in two sales in August 1922 and March 1923 the Earl of Craven put on the market the rest of his Craven Arms estate, including, in the 1923 sale, the Craven Arms Hotel. In both cases the land was advertised as comprising "valuable building sites suitable for business premises, factories, etc." and areas "situate amidst picturesque surroundings, suitable for the erection of residences, villas or cottages." The 1923 sale map showed as laid out for housing development the land at the bottom of the Clun Road, strips beside the Shrewsbury and Corvedale Roads, and the fields where Mayfield Avenue, the car park, playing field and Newington Way now are. Much of the property was bought either by Jackson and McCartney for their business or by H. S. McCartney for the family, but the fields to the back of Shrewsbury Road and Corvedale Road did not reach their reserve price and were withdrawn, coming finally on the market in 1935. The People's Refreshment House Association bought the Craven Arms Hotel (for £9,000), while some local businessmen, for example George Gornall, described by Kelly's Directory in the 1920s as "a painter" of Market Street, and William Nicholas, a draper, outfitter and house furnisher, of Manchester House, Market Street, also acquired land.

Despite the withdrawal of the Craven Estate from most of its interest in Craven Arms, private development of property continued only slowly – there is a date of 1926 on Craven House next to the former Post Office building in the Shrewsbury Road, Craven Lodge opposite was built in 1930, being a model of the 1929 Ideal Home Exhibition House, while much further north Sibdon View has

A larger version of this map appears inside the back cover

the date of 1934 and the initials of its builder, W. H. Miller. But in 1926 the Parish Council entered the field, and a new stage in the development of the town began.

In January of that year the Council approached the London Midland and Scottish Railway and the Great Western Railway to ask whether they could "do anything in the building of houses in Craven Arms". The context suggests that it was an increase in railway staff "on appointments" which was the cause of concern. At the same time a letter was sent to the District Council asking them to find a solution to the problem. It was to be the District Council who took action, for by January 1930 twenty two houses were ready for letting (only four went to people from outside Craven Arms) just to the north of the Clun Road. The road in which what were called the parlour type houses stood was to be called Greenfields Road and that of the non-parlour type Meadow Road. It was at this point that the condition of and responsibility for what was then called Gas House Lane, subsequently renamed Brook Road, which led to some of the new housing, first came to the fore, to recur periodically for the next seventy years. More houses were added in this area in 1933 and 1934.

The period of stability in the town's population from the years before the first World War to the 1950s was matched by a similar lack of substantial change in the character of its trades, businesses and services

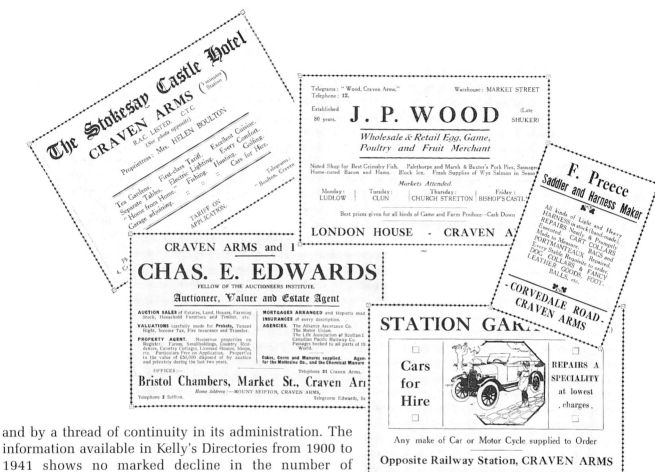

and by a thread of continuity in its administration. The information available in Kelly's Directories from 1900 to 1941 shows no marked decline in the number of commercial entries – the total being in the seventies throughout the period, with about forty shops of various kinds, ten or so tradesmen (blacksmith, carpenter, mason), a dozen offering professional services (the doctors, veterinary surgeon and so on) and a similar number services of a more general nature, like hotels and refreshment rooms. Over these years and beyond a number of people served long periods on the Parish Council: among them were W. Davies, who was 26 years on the Council and chairman for 16 years in the 1920s and 1930s; W. Phillips, a councillor for 37 years from 1925, was chairman for ten years from 1936 to 1946, while W. D. Griffiths served as councillor from 1925 to 1966, with 14 years as chairman (their modern equivalent is Councillor Stephens, who was first elected in 1970). There have also been two long serving clerks – J. Chester, who was Parish Clerk for 30 years in the Council's earliest days, and H. H. Elkes, who served for almost 29 years from 1954.

Of course, there were some changes which reflected the changing times. In 1909 the Stokesay Castle Hotel was listed as having a motor garage and inspection pit and by 1913 there were three garages in the town. More exotic was the cycle agent – A. Maund and Company's Central Cycle and Motor Depot of Market Street, with a branch in Station Road. His 1910 bill-head, beside a picture of an early bi-plane, advertised the Company as "Agents for all the best makes of Cars, Motor Cycles and Cycles", continuing "Aeroplanes Supplied and Repaired. All kinds of repairs executed. Accumulators

The Shrewsbury Cooperative Society at the corner of Dale Street and Newton Street, 1912

Craven Arms station with J.C. Edge's timber businesses in the foreground

charged. Motor Cars and Motor Cycles for Hire. Mailcarts, Bassinettes, Phonographs, Records and all accessories in stock." Craven Arms had to wait until 1935 for a cinema, the Regal, whose proprietor, J. N. Robson, also ran the County Motor and Engineering Company (now Craven Cars) and built a number of other cinemas in the district – the first advertisement in the Shrewsbury Chronicle of Friday December 6 1935, read REGAL CINEMA, CRAVEN ARMS. The Luxury Cinema of South Shropshire. Today Ronald Colman in 'The Masquerader' Cert. A. Also a Thriller Western 'When a Man sees Red'. The cinema screened advertisements for local businesses: "Don't go down the mine, dad. Buy it from Summerfield and Co." and "Every morning when you rise put on one of Salmon's ties." are two which remain in local memories.

Larger scale businesses came slowly to the town. By 1912 Stubbs and Co., later to be Stubbs, Meeson and Co., Corn Merchants and Millers, were doing business from the Market Hall. In 1912 J. C. Edge and Co. set up a timber business and sawmill on a greenfield site just to the west of the station off Brook Road; the business was to develop into Bendware, making, for a national and international market, top quality tennis and badminton rackets, billiard cues, cricket bats – the Walter Hammond range -, and Victor Barna table tennis bats (Victor Barna came on one occasion in the late 1930s and played exhibition games in the Craven Arms Hotel Ballroom against the local Boys Club). In the early 1920s South Shropshire Farmers Ltd. started to trade as wool buyers, corn, seed and manure merchants in the Shrewsbury Road beyond the station; and by the mid 1930s Samuel Spencer was trading as timber merchant and haulage contractor in Newington at the northern end of the town.

The principal element in the town's business, apart from but linked with its function as a railway junction, continued, as it had done from the late 1870s, to be the stock markets. There were sales of cattle by auction every alternate Monday and of horses monthly. A surviving sales catalogue for the sale of 250 heavy horses by Jackson and McCartney at the South Shropshire and Central Wales Horse Repository on Saturday 4 March 1911 advised vendors that "Horses described as 'good workers', 'having been worked', 'used to all farm work', 'quiet in all gears', 'suitable for town work', or other description in the opinion of the Auctioneers calculated to convey the impression that the horses are capable of reasonable work, shall constitute a warranty that the same are quiet and capable of working."

SOUTH SHROPSHIRE AND CENTRAL WALES

HORSE REPOSITORY,

CRAVEN ARMS, SALOP.

Judging at 10·30

Sale Commences at 11·30 prompt

Judging the Cart Geldings and Mares at a Recent Sale.

CATALOGUE of PRIZE SALE of

250 HORSES

SATURDAY NEXT, MARCH 4th, 1911.

MESSRS JACKSON & McCARTNEY. Auctioneers.

A winter horse sale about 1940

Furthermore "A SHIVERER cannot be classed as a good worker, or sold as sound. A CRIB-BITER, WIND-SUCKER OR RIG must be so described in the catalogue. A SHIVERER costing 20 guineas or over is returnable unless stated at the time of the sale."

But the great events, as had been the case for the predecessors of the firm of Jackson and McCartney since 1875, were the late summer sheep sales. To take examples over a period of forty years, Jackson and McCartney auctioned 17,000 sheep on Thursday 27 August 1908, 22,000 on Thursday 30 August 1928 and 14,000 on Thursday 26 August 1948. At the same time of the year the firm of Morris, Marshall, and Poole (later Morris, Barker and Poole) held their annual sheep auction in Craven Arms also disposing of very large numbers of sheep. To take 1928 as an example, on 5 September they sold 20,000 sheep "mostly drafts from the upland flocks of the district in very sound condition." And these were followed a week or so later by supplementary sales by both firms. But they were not the only sales in the area. In 1944 Morris, Barker and Poole's Annual Sale catalogue advertised sales of 70,000 sheep from late August to early October at Ludlow, Craven Arms and Knighton (twice) and a single sale at Church Stretton. Prizes were awarded for the best pens of Kerry Hill, Clun Forest and Shropshire sheep (the Kerry Hill stock book had started in 1899 and the Clun Forest in the early 1920s).

The impact of these auctions upon Craven Arms can be imagined from the newspaper accounts of the sales in 1908 and 1928. "The Largest Ewe Sale in England. On Thursday 27 August [1908] Messrs. Jackson and McCartney of Craven Arms and Ludlow held their 34th great annual sale of stock ewes and rams. The penning commenced shortly after 5 a.m. and by 9 o'clock the enormous number of 17,000 head of sheep were in their places. A large complement of buyers were in attendance from all parts of the United Kingdom, and no difficulty was experienced by them in securing what they required out of so large a collection, which comprised about 5,000 prize-bred Shropshire Down ewes, 10,500 Clun Forest, Kerry Hill and Longmynd and improved cross-bred ewes, 2,000 yearling wethers and lambs and 70 Shropshire Down, Oxford Down, Hampshire Down, Kerry Hill and Longmynd rams....The trade from the start was very good and there was very keen demand for the Shropshires. The trade for the rams was far in excess of last year. Three sales rings were going at the same time, commencing with the Shropshires in No. 1 ring. The cross-breds were dealt with in No. 2 ring, beginning at 10 o'clock prompt, and the rams in No. 3 ring at 1 o'clock." The 1928 report added other details. "The entry [22,000] constituted the finest collection of breeds of the locality which it is possible for this essentially sheep producing district to muster and the distinction of it being the largest ewe sale in England being upheld. The sale attracted a large gathering of buyers, many being present who have attended the sale for years past, which testifies to the excellent results they have obtained. They are unanimous that the sheep from these parts invariably improve and give satisfaction wherever they go. A keen demand was experienced throughout the sale, trade, as anticipated, showing an improvement on last year's prices. This resulted in a complete clearance being effected, over 320 truck loads

Jackson and McCartney's summer ewe sale

of sheep being dispatched by rail, while many thousands were driven by road."

The dispatch of such huge numbers of sheep from the auction fields (Jackson and McCartney's was between the Craven Arms Hotel and the station on the west side of the Shrewsbury road, Morris, Marshall and Poole's on the area to the north of the Corvedale Road and to the east of the Shrewsbury Road) was a substantial logistical exercise. Mr John McCartney, a partner in the firm, remembers telephoning the station master before the sales in the 1950s to ask for 250 or more wagons (each held 40 sheep) to be made available. But while very many went out by rail, and increasingly later by road, the great majority were walked in.

The list of successful sales in the 1908 Shrewsbury Chronicle or Morris, Barker and Poole's 1944 catalogue of vendors is a roll call of the farms of south-west Shropshire, each offering one or more lots of from 10 to 60 sheep. A typical page in the catalogue gave Edenhope, Abdon, Stanton Long, Merrivale, Whitbatch, Broadstone, Brampton, Vron End, The Cwm, Purslow, Bucknell, Beckjay and Hopton Heath. For these great sales all roads led to Craven Arms and all were full of sheep. Brian Morgan remembers how in the 1930s his father, Melville Morgan of The Llan in the hills above Clunbury, would move his ewes for sale down to Crowsmoor, on the road between Aston-on-Clun and Long Meadow End, on the day before the sale, so that farmers from further up the Clun Valley, who could not have driven their sheep from home to Craven Arms before the sale began, could lodge their flocks overnight at The Llan and, with a 6 o'clock start, be into town in time for the sale. Each flock had a man in front and a man behind with their dogs, and they came down the valley nose to tail, so that a farmer bringing his flock in at Little Brampton, Beambridge or Long Meadow End might have to wait ten minutes or more for a gap to get in.

These years of stability in the life of the town were also years of stability in the school. After its first 40 years of frequent changes in staff, between 1890 and 1950 the school had only two headmasters – Thomas Mountford from 1890 until 1925, when he retired because of failing eyesight, and David Davies – and Mr Davies' successor in 1950, Ivan Kennedy, was to stay for 24 years. Other members of staff stayed for long periods. For example Miss Bewick came in 1900 and taught the infants class until 1936, while Mrs Jukes joined the staff in 1922 and retired in 1957 and Mrs Thomas had thirty five years at the school from 1933 to 1968. Numbers in the school climbed from about 150 in the early 1920s to around 170 in 1925 (Halford School was closed in 1924), and occasionally neared the 200 mark during the decade before the Second War. From Mr Mountford's time onwards children from the school (an all-age school through to 14) were regularly successful in winning places to go on to the Grammar Schools in Ludlow and, later, the senior schools in Shrewsbury. Mr Mountford's son, also Thomas, was the first of these in 1909. Critical Inspection reports, a feature of the

Please bring this Catalogue with you.

CRAVEN ARMS
SHROPSHIRE,
on the Shrewsbury and Hereford Railway.

CATALOGUE of the Breeders' Great Annual Sale of Kerry Hill, Clun Forest and Cross-bred Sheep
COMPRISING ABOUT

16,000
GRAND YOUNG EWES
and STORE LAMBS,
AND A SELECTION OF
Kerry Hill & Hampshire Rams & Ram Lambs
To be sold at CRAVEN ARMS, in a Field opposite the Railway Station,

on THURSDAY, SEPT. 7th, 1944
Commencing at 10-45 a.m.

AUCTIONEERS
MORRIS, BARKER & POOLE

Catalogues may be obtained from the Auctioneers' Head Office, Ludlow (Tel. 53), Shropshire.

COMMISSIONS FAITHFULLY EXECUTED.

1880s, disappeared. The report of 1937 gives a good impression of the sort of education that was being offered.

"This is a well run school, providing for 177 children ranging from four to fourteen years of age, and organised in five classes. The Head Master's careful and thorough teaching of the top class and his systematic and sensible supervision of the rest of the school result in much effective work being done in the various subjects in the curriculum. The children are pleasant and willing and acquire habits of industry as they pass through the school. The formal subjects of reading, writing and arithmetic are dealt with effectively, and have benefited from an increased use of group work. Speech training is helped by Dramatization, and a freer use of literature has had a beneficial effect on written English. During the past two years handwork has made good progress both as regards basketry in Class 3 and weaving in Class 2, and it should be noted that facilities for the instruction of senior boys in woodwork have been provided since the date of the last report. The water colour work of the top class, mainly depicting still life, deserves high commendation. In History and Geography lessons a knowledge of facts is looked for and obtained, although there is some weakness in this respect in Class 2. In the top class the syllabus in History is perhaps too exclusively concerned with political History and it is suggested that some training of the older children to study independently from books might be introduced. The infants who are sensibly taught in a cheerful room, are vivacious and happy, and make marked general progress."

The Log Books illuminate the advances in public health provision which were made from the 1880s onwards. Epidemics of various kinds often closed the school – measles could be especially virulent, four children in the parish dying in the epidemic of 1869 – but the decision to close in those days was a matter for the managers. Dr Tredinnick came to Craven Arms in 1885 and the school was closed "on doctor's orders" for the whole of March 1886 when there was an especially severe outbreak of measles in the district, while in December 1889 "Dr. Thursfield, the Medical Officer of the district, strongly recommended the closing of the school and offered a medical certificate proving the prevalence of contagious sore throat in Craven Arms and the danger of permitting children from Aldon (sore throat) from entering the school." Influenza also took its

Stokesay schoolchildren c. 1930. Mr Davies, the headmaster is on the left.

toll. In 1904 "the school was closed the whole of last week owing to the illness of the two assistants, especially the dangerous illness of Mrs Mountford, which necessitated the absence of Mr Mountford, the Head Master. Mrs Mountford died on Wednesday 17 March."

In November 1908 regular annual health inspections began and in 1914 a school nurse was appointed, the first being Miss M. La Touche. 1919 brought the first dental inspections to the school and in 1925 eye inspections were instituted; in the town a dentist was in attendance once a week from at least 1926, but an optician, also providing a weekly service, did not gain mention in Kelly's Directory until 1937. A local community nurse had been appointed in 1904 by the "Onnyside Nursing Association" but the first incumbent, Nurse Murray, stayed only a short while; she was replaced by Nurse Folke, who, according to the Parochial Magazine of March 1905, had taken the same room at Strefford "which place is found to be very central for the district". By 1913 Mrs Mary Williams was the midwife, living in Newton Street. One of her successors, as District Nurse, Mrs Rosa Buckley M. B. E., was to spend more than forty years in post, before retiring in January 1975. At her retirement it was estimated that she had travelled 250,000 miles in the course of her duties and delivered more than 3,000 babies.

Of the other social services in the town the Post Office had moved up in 1879 from Newton, where the wheelwright, William Jones, had been the post master, to Thomas Groves' new house in Corvedale Road, where he and his widow, Elizabeth looked after the postal services until the 1890s. By 1895 Edwin Thomas was post master, an office he combined with his business as corn dealer, which he ran from Bristol House – now the charity shop on the corner of Dale Street and Market Street – for over twenty years, being succeeded by George Corbett. He retired in 1938 after 45 years in the postal service in Craven Arms, his father and uncle also being local postmen before him. During the 1920s and 1930s the post office was located in a wooden building in Corvedale Road next to the Methodist Church. After sustained pressure from the Parish Council which started in 1926, this was finally replaced in 1940 by the purpose built building in the Shrewsbury Road. When, in 1974, the G.P.O. withdrew the counter services from there, the Parish Clerk expressed his dismay at seeing "this building, a source of pride to this small township, closed after 30 years."

In the town's early days the police constable was in Newton and down to 1909 a succession of officers were described as 'constable in charge'. In 1913, however, George Lovatt was sergeant in charge, which suggests that additional officers were under his command, a supposition confirmed by the 1922 directory entry: "Police Station. Walter Frost, sergeant in charge and 4 constables." At some time before this the police station had moved into the Clun Road by Albion Terrace. Perhaps the increase in the police

Bristol House at the corner of Dale Street and Market Street

complement derived from representations made by the Parish Council in December 1910, when they agreed that a resolution should be sent to the Chief Constable of Salop. "that this council is of the opinion that additional police supervision should be granted to Craven Arms having regard to the following facts. The frequency of auctions of cattle and horses and other stock sales. The immense amount of vehiculared [*sic*] and motor traffic passing through this busy centre to the Railway Station and other places. The population of about 1,200 within the radius of one mile from the Craven Arms Market Hall. Also the large amount of casuals passing through the neighbourhood." Nonetheless there is little evidence from the Council Minutes or from contemporary newspapers that the maintenance of law and order presented much problem in Craven Arms during these years.

In 1926 the first fire brigade was enrolled: A. E. Andrews, Corvedale Road, J. Evans, Railway Terrace, C. Harper, Albion Terrace, G. Jones, Newton, W. Jones, Clun Road, A. Lucas, Clun Road, J. Reeves, Newton, N. Salmon, Corvedale Road, S. Stead, Newton Green, and C. Terry, Newton Street. Harper was appointed captain, to be succeeded by Stead in 1927, but it was three months before the brigade, on the pressing of the Parish Council, attended for practice, for which each man was paid 1/- [5p] with 2/- [10p] for the captain. A fire earned them 2/6 [12½p] per man and 5/- [25p] for the captain.

Craven Arms Fire Brigade in the 1950s

The School Log Books also provide glimpses of other aspects of life in the community, often through mention of school attendance being down because of the children's absence at some function or other. On 24 May 1866 a large number of children were away at 'the Newton Club Feast', while on the same day in 1876 the entry read "No school owing to there being a Club walk in the village". In 1877 the day's record was simply "Holiday – there being a large fair and Club Walk at Craven Arms." These early entries have a double significance.

First they draw attention to the Clubs or Friendly Societies which were formed to provide help to those of their members who were in financial difficulties through sickness or disability without their having to resort to poor relief with its prospect of the Union Workhouse. This did not always prove possible and the records of the Ludlow Union for 1851 recorded four people who were on poor relief as also receiving weekly payments from their Club – the amounts were small, usually 2/- [10p] weekly. The Census of that year (the only year in which the Stokesay Census provided the information) showed twenty five people in the parish of Stokesay receiving poor relief out of a population of 529 (that is, 4.7%, compared with the national average of 5.75%). Most of them were the very elderly or widows with small children, and the largest number lived at Whettleton Common. By comparison there were four people in the parish on poor relief in 1899 in a population of about 1,000 (far below the national average in 1900 of 2.5%) and seven in 1918. The Newton Club perhaps dated from 1841, when the Quarter Sessions roll for 18 October recorded that the rules of "the Newton Friendly Society" were allowed. By 1879 a Craven Arms Branch of the Manchester Unity of the Independent Order of Oddfellows was in existence, as well as the Newton Club, and in the 1890s the Ancient Order of Foresters appeared. As late as July 1932 the Oddfellows' and Foresters' trips closed the school for the day.

What was involved in one of these Societies' annual celebrations was described in a report of 2 June 1894 in the Ludlow Advertiser of the Anniversary Celebration of the Court Longville Castle of the Ancient Order of Foresters, Shrewsbury District. 120 members met at the Court Room in the Lion Inn and, preceded by the Shropshire Artillery Band, marched with banners flying to Halford Church for divine service. After that they paraded through the "principal thoroughfares" to Penlu House (in Clun Road, the residence of their chairman, Dr Tredinnick). They then returned to the Market Hall to a "most substantial dinner, served by Mr. Spriggins, of the Lion Inn, Newton" followed by equally substantial speeches. Mr Morris, the secretary, reported that in the previous year the Court had paid out £102 for sickness; its funds stood at £785 5s 11½d [£785.30p]; there were 143 adult members and 53 juveniles.

Secondly the entries record the earliest mention of the event which was to become the Craven Arms May Fair – it was occasionally called the Craven Arms Annual Pleasure Fair. This was held on the field opposite the Craven Arms Hotel on the corner of Corvedale Road and the Ludlow Road and took place annually on or about 24 May – Queen Victoria's birthday, a date shared, in the first thirty years or so of the twentieth century, with the celebration of Empire Day, which in its early days was an occasion at the school for patriotic songs and an address by the School Master on the "Greatness of the Empire". It usually involved the school being closed for the day – the last mention of a holiday specifically for the Fair was in 1954 (although in 1965 an 'occasional' holiday was given on that day). In 1925 the Fair took place on Monday 25 May and the following day's entry by Mr Davies read, "Most of the children were on the fairground until after midnight and are very sleepy."

This was not the only outside event to impinge upon the school's routine. Down to 1900 the involvement of some of the children in rural activities – such as haymaking, mushroom, blackberry and potato picking – was always likely to affect attendance. The date of the summer holiday tended to be fixed by the timing of the harvest; for example, a late harvest in 1884 saw the holiday start on 2 September and end on 30 September. But after 1906 absence for these purposes was rarely mentioned (some children were back late from the summer holiday in 1922 because of whinberry picking) until the 1939 – 45 War when children regularly helped with potato picking. While the call of the fields might have been diminishing as the twentieth century began, the summer brought other events which took the children out of school. Throughout the first twenty years of the century, the Sunday School treats of all the chapels and churches made inroads into school attendance, sometimes to the extent that the school decided to cut its losses and close for the day: 1 August 1906 "More than half the school children are attending Sunday School Treats given by the Primitive Methodists and Plymouth Brethren"; 23 July 1919 "The Church Sunday School Treat.

School closed."

These events indicate the vigour of the churches in the town during these years. Within ten years of its establishment the Primitive Methodist Chapel set up a children's class and in 1890 funds were raised to extend the chapel. The Church of England Mission Church in Corvedale Road was quickly into its stride, establishing a Sunday School in March 1896 with 40 children and four teachers; by the end of 1897 the number had increased to 136. In 1905 there were services of Holy Communion, matins, and evensong every Sunday, and a children's afternoon service as well. The register of services at the church which survives for the years 1916 to 1943 shows that the Church had a regular congregation throughout those years, though there seem to have been few services other than Holy Communion from the 1920s onwards – 286 communicants during 1918 with 16 on Christmas Day, 404 in 1928 with 32 on Christmas Day, 280 in 1938 with 19 on Christmas Day, dropping to 112 in 1943 with 14 on Christmas Day. In 1909 the Wesleyan Methodists moved from Longville into Craven Arms. They were able to buy a plot of land from the Earl of Craven in Corvedale Road in 1910 and, after some deliberation about the quality of building (it was first planned to be of corrugated iron), the new chapel was built and opened on 11 September 1913. The initials of the prime movers in the scheme are to be seen on a stone plaque in the wall dated 1913: they were Albert C. Torr, a railwayman, Edward (Ted) Medlicott, also a railwayman, and George H. Brown, a carpenter and builder.

The town's social activities were, however, broadly based. From its earliest days the large room above the Market Hall – the "new" Assembly room of 1889 – provided a venue for a wide variety of events: public meetings, concerts by the Craven Arms Male Voice Choir, a predecessor of the present Craven Arms Men's Chorus, Hunt Balls, dinners, the Women's Institute Show (the Craven Arms W. I. was founded in 1919) and even the occasional boxing match. From the late 1930s onwards the ballroom and banqueting room at the Craven Arms Hotel became the venue for this sort of function. The British Legion Club began its life in Craven Arms in a building behind the Market Hall, before moving down to the former Baptist Chapel in the late 1920s and then across the Ludlow Road to its present site in the 1930s, ultimately changing its name to the Craven Arms Services Social and Sports Club in 1951. The Baptist Chapel served in a number of other capacities after this. It provided a much needed youth club in the 1930s, led by one of the local policemen of the time, P. C. Hemmings; it became the British Restaurant in 1942 and after that gave canteen facilities for the school. It is now a private house. On the Corvedale Road (next to Barclays Bank) was the Railwaymen's Social Club – the Railwaymen's Hut.

The Railwaymen's Hut

Craven Arms Cricket team 1937

Sport was also a feature of the town's life. The school log book for May 1902 mentioned the Craven Arms Horticultural Show "at which there were sports", while on 6 July 1905 the children "through the kindness of Mr Hartshorn [landlord of the Stokesay Castle Hotel] were enabled to gain admission to the cricket and sports and were entertained by a good tea at the expense of Mr. F. W. Barnes." Again, in 1910, there was entertainment on "The Cricket Field". The Cricket Club – a successor to one which had existed earlier in the nineteenth century – was founded by Dr. Tredinnick and Mr. Herbert Allcroft in 1891. In the 1930s the Craven Arms Cricket Club played on a field, with pavilion, across the Onny at Newton, which belonged to Mr. Meddins of Whettleton. In February 1908 the Air Gun Club held a social and dance for 170 people at the Market Hall, the entertainment continuing until 3 a.m., reported the Ludlow Advertiser and Craven Arms Gazette. The formation of Air Gun Clubs was a phenomenon of the first decade of the twentieth century – there was an Air Gun League in the Clun Valley and both Clunbury School and Bishop's Castle School are known to have possessed and practised with air guns in these years. Between the Wars there was also a flourishing and successful Football Club, which played on a field to the north of Corvedale Road, where the Council houses were subsequently built; a Bowls Club on Newton Green; a Hockey Club, with both men's and women's teams, playing on a meadow at the top end of Brook Road; and a Tennis Club, formed in May 1935, with courts by the Stokesay Castle Hotel. In 1937, the Secretary of the Bowls Club was Roger Blakeway, of the Cricket Club Roy Reynolds, of the Football Club Charlie Farr, and of the Hockey Club Hayden Francis. All of these, except Charlie Farr, who was a railwayman, were connected with Jackson and McCartney.

Craven Arms Football Club 1923

6: THE POST WAR YEARS

For the forty years since 1900 the development of Craven Arms' early years had been sustained; it was a bustling and lively place, its broadly balanced economy providing not only for its own residents but making it a focus for the villages around it. Up to this point four principal themes ran through the story of its development – the railway junction as a provider of work, with the consequent growth in population, the junction as a focus for the livestock trade of the area, the availability of land for the developing community, and the provision of facilities to service that community. But in the years after 1945 that was to change. Already two inter-related factors, which were universal across the country, were starting to have their local effect – the growth of road traffic both for the transport of goods and for personal travel and, in consequence, the gradual decline of the railway. At first the pace of change was slow and the signs of it perceptible perhaps only with hindsight. From the mid-1920s the Parish Council's minutes reveal growing concerns about traffic on the A49 and at its junctions by the Craven Arms Hotel – danger for children crossing, the difficulties of the corner by the milestone obelisk, and problems at the railway bridge on the Clun Road, not least of periodic flooding. In 1935 the Bishop's Castle Railway finally succumbed to the forces of economic necessity and breathed its last. At the time that may not have seemed all that significant – after all from its earliest days the railway had struggled to keep its head above the waters of terminal insolvency – but it was in fact the first step along the road which over the next thirty five years led to a fundamental change in the character of Craven Arms.

The start of war in 1939 had an immediate, but not a permanent, effect upon the town. Mr Davies wrote: "Owing to the outbreak of War School did not open until 9 a.m. today Monday 11 Sept. As the school has to be used by our own children and the children of Gwladys Street Council School, Liverpool [by Goodison Park, the home of Everton Football Club] we are compelled to work a double shift system at School. This week Stokesay children are attending school in the mornings from 9 – 12.30 and the Liverpool children in the afternoon." Ten days later he recorded: "The two top classes will put in 9 half days, Standards II and III will put in 9 half days, Standard I 8 half days and the Infants Class 5 half days. These are actual school attendances and when a class is not in school it will be engaged in work either at the Mission Church or the Boy's Club [the Baptist Chapel] under the direction of its teacher. In addition the woodwork room is available for use for two afternoons of the week, so that but for the Infant Class the school will be run as nearly full time as possible and the ordinary syllabus of work will be covered as far as it can be done." At the beginning the evacuees were organised into four classes, soon reduced to three when one of the Liverpool teachers left, and in May 1940 the two schools merged. Mr Davies did not give the original number of evacuees, but in April 1941 recorded the school numbers as 159 Shropshire children, 44 Private evacuees and 37 Official evacuees. Their numbers gradually declined over the next three years, 6 being present in August 1944 – the last mention of them.

There was also a substantial military presence in the town and the neighbourhood. The Grove was occupied, the Temperance Hotel was requisitioned, a cluster of huts went up at the eastern end of Corvedale Road on both sides, and the military used other buildings in the town – the School in the holidays, the Mission Church and the Primitive Methodist chapel.

Home Guard

As the War drew towards its conclusion Mr W. D. Griffiths proposed that the Council should immediately "formulate a scheme of post-war planning to build at least 20 more houses and suggested as a suitable site the football ground and allotments". A letter was sent to the District Council to this effect. There had been scattered building along the eastern edge of the Shrewsbury Road going north and some sporadic development of various sorts on the north side of the Corvedale Road, but this was the first time that a larger part of the area bounded by these two roads and the river in the east had been suggested for housing. But in the event the next tranches of council houses were additions to the estate to the west of the railway in 1947 and 1952.

It was not until the latter part of the 1960s, reflected in a very substantial increase in the population in that decade (1961 – 1217: 1971 – 1463) that the site to the north of Corvedale Road was substantially developed, while in 1970 a start was made on the Newington Estate. Throughout the 1970s the need for more housing was a regular issue before the Council, but now the solution was to be found, as it had been in the town's earliest days, in private development, first in the early 1980s on the site of J. C. Edge's former saw mill and factory, between the railway and Brook Road, later on land belonging to C. P. Wood at the top of Greenfields Road, and on the auction field site between the railway and Shrewsbury Road which McCartneys had acquired from the Craven Estate in 1923 and is now White Meadow Close.

After the war the scars left by the army took a while to erase. The Primitive Methodist Chapel, unlike some of the other buildings, remained in adequate repair, but its congregation was in decline and in 1960 it closed its doors and amalgamated with the Wesleyan Methodist church in Corvedale Road (itself to be extended with a Sunday School and Church Hall in 1964). The old chapel in Market Street was bought by J. P. Wood and Sons and in 1961 it was given by the family to the Catholic Community in Craven Arms and district as St Andrew's Church to perpetuate the memory of their mother and father, Jane and John P. Wood. The Mission Church (the 'Tin Church') in Corvedale Road was coming to the end of its life and in 1946 the Stokesay Parochial Church Council decided that it was not worth refurbishing for services. For a while it became the Church Hall but once a new Church Youth Club (St. Christopher's) was built next door, it fell into disuse, rapidly became dilapidated and was sold for £100 to Norbury P. C. C. in 1950. Also in Corvedale Road seven of the old army huts were converted and used as council homes until their demolition in 1954, while others, on the north side, were occupied by squatters. The fate of the Temperance Hotel took much longer to unfold.

The Army did not leave it until March 1951, but before then consideration was being given to its public acquisition and conversion for additional housing. Once that idea was abandoned on grounds of cost in 1953 attention turned to its future use. The question was bedeviled by the fact that nobody, to begin with, knew the true history of the building and it took some years and protracted consultation with the Charity Commissioners to sort out. The Craven Arms Reading Room and Coffee House Trust had to be revived and negotiations opened with the Earl of Craven, who owned the freehold, and with the War Department about dilapidations caused during the army's occupation of the building. Eventually, after the ninety nine year lease under which the building had been taken from the Earl of Craven came to its end in 1963 and the negotiated compensation of £1,500 had been paid to the Earl of Craven, the building was sold to a private owner in 1965. At the Annual Parish Meeting in 1969 it was reported that the money remaining in the Trust had been made available to the Craven Arms Playing Field Association, partly as a lump sum and partly as a capital endowment to be applied to the upkeep and maintenance of the playing fields.

The Primitive Methodist Chapel in course of conversion to the Catholic Church

The need for a public playing field and children's recreation ground in the town first appeared as an issue for the Parish Council in 1948. In 1923 the Allcroft family had leased the triangle of land between the brook and Ludlow Road where Lambeth Close now stands as a recreation area for children, but in 1938 the lease was ended; while all of the town's sports clubs played on fields which were also leased from private owners. The need for a sports and recreation facility was periodically raised during the 1950s, but without resolution. In 1960 Messrs R. R. and S. W. McCartney offered for sale one of their fields in the Shrewsbury Road and in February 1961 the Craven Arms Playing Fields Association was established to raise money to buy the sports field, to erect a pavilion and for other amenities including a children's play area. An appeal was launched in the summer of that year and the field purchased in 1963.

During the discussions in the 1950s of what to do with any proceeds from the disposal of the Temperance Hotel the possibility of their being used to help finance the provision of a public meeting place in the town was raised. Apart from the upper room in the Market Hall the town had never had this facility – and did not do so, despite the disused Market Hall and the Cinema being considered by the Council as possibilities in the 1960s, until the Community Centre was opened some forty years later – but at the time local people thought that a playing field was a more pressing requirement, not least because there were plans afoot for the development of the school, which would have offered a purpose built hall for the town to use. This was not to be.

In the years immediately after the Second War primary and secondary education was reorganised in South Shropshire, with the intention of replacing the all-age schools with a two tier, primary (5 – 11) and secondary (11+), system – an arrangement which had begun elsewhere in the 1920s but came late to many rural areas. Stokesay School was planned to have a key role in this. Children of 11 – 14 were gradually to be transferred to Stokesay from schools in the immediate neighbourhood. When this process was complete and the small village schools were all converted to primary schools, Craven Arms was to get its own purpose built secondary modern school, on a site at the top of Greenfields Road. The first group of 27 children from outside the town appeared in January 1947 and when the school leaving age was raised to 15 in March that year the school took on the 14 – 15 year olds from Clunbury, Clungunford, Culmington, Diddlebury, Edgton, Hopesay, Munslow, and Onibury Church of England Schools. The Onibury over 11s came in 1949 and most years in the 1950s brought additional seniors from other schools (1958, for example, saw "a new intake of 25 seniors", who were from Clunbury). By October 1960 there were three hundred children on the school's roll. But in 1961 the plan for a modern school at Craven Arms was shelved by the Shropshire Education Committee. Despite vigorous local protests and the support of Jasper More, the local M.P., and Sir Philip Magnus-Allcroft, the Education Committee's decision was upheld on appeal by the full County Council and in July 1962 by the Minister of Education. At the end of the summer term in 1964 60 seniors and juniors left for secondary schools, either at Church Stretton or at Ludlow; "All told a sad occasion for the school" wrote Mr Kennedy. A few seniors stayed on but in July 1966 Mr Kennedy observed "From next term the school will have no senior scholars. The end of an era." The school was organised as a primary school with four classes and the staff was reduced to five. In 1983 a nursery unit originally for 40 was opened and then during 1986,1987 and 1988 a major redevelopment and extension of the school was undertaken, which included a new hall, a children's library and a branch of the Shropshire County Library. Finally in 1994 the nursery and reception were housed in a new building over the road in Newton. At present the school roll is just over 200, plus 50 in the nursery.

One other building occupied by the army in the 1939/45 war was to play an important role in the life of Craven Arms in the last fifty years. In 1949 the Grove Estate in Wistanstow was sold and in 1954 the Victorian mansion was demolished. Soon afterwards in 1956 the site was bought by the firm of J. P. Wood and Sons, which had begun its life in 1888 at London House in Market Street as a shop purveying game, poultry, fish and fruit owned by James Overton. In 1913 his daughter, Jane, married John P. Wood, himself the grandson of Mary Shuker of Horderley who had started a poultry business in 1834. After J. P. Wood's death in 1924 Mrs Wood carried on the business, later with the help of her four sons, until her death in 1943, developing both its retail and wholesale trade around the district. From 1956 the Woods built up on the

Grove site one of the largest poultry businesses in the country, trading, together with Dale Turkeys of Caynham, as Midland Poultry Holdings. By the late 1970s, it was processing some 500,000 chickens a week and distributing them nationwide in their lorry fleet, marked with its distinctive trade name 'Chukie Chickens'. They were the major employer in the area with some 1,500 in all, 700 of whom were at The Grove, when they were at their busiest. In 1968 the business was sold to Unilever and, after passing to Unigate it was closed on the Grove site in the early 1990s.

J.P. Wood's shop, London House, Market Street

The growth of this business over the twenty years or so after 1956 and the employment it provided served to soften the impact of what could otherwise have been a shattering blow to the town's economy and its life.

From 31 December 1951 the passenger service on the Much Wenlock line was withdrawn; goods trains had run on the line only 'when required' for several years previously. This went unremarked in the Parish Council minutes, but British Rail's later plans for what in 1959 was euphemistically called "modernisation" did not. The Council meeting in October 1957 noted the receipt of a letter from the British Transport Commission about the proposed withdrawal of facilities from twelve stations on the Shrewsbury to Hereford line, which left just Church Stretton, Craven Arms and Stokesay, Ludlow and Leominster. Five years later came the first threat to the Central Wales Railway. To the amazement of the Stokesay Council the Ludlow Rural District Council did not at first oppose this. After a public enquiry in October 1962 the line was reprieved in 1964 for passengers services. That year saw the last of the through freight services on the line, next year local freight services ceased, and between October 1965 and March 1966 the line to Knighton reverted to its original single track. Once more, in 1968, the Parish Council was exercised by a further proposal to remove passenger services from the line, but again the proposal was dropped. In the meantime the "modernisation" of the main line had continued.

In March 1967 British Rail Western Region announced plans for withdrawing from Ludlow and Craven Arms facilities for general merchandise traffic, which would be handled for the future at Hereford, and in April 1968 the local Western Region freight service was withdrawn. From 1968 the station buildings were gradually demolished to be followed by the engine shed. The only signal box retained was the one at the Long Lane Crossing; the station box had closed in 1956 and the one at the Central Wales junction in 1965. The consequential withdrawal of railway staff brought the demolition of Newington Terrace and part of Railway Terrace in 1970. Complaints from the Council in 1968 about the lack of facilities at the station received the response that "Now that staff had been withdrawn from the two stations [which the other was is not clear] any removable furniture had to be removed to escape attention by vandals. Their policy was for existing buildings on unstaffed stations to be demolished and replaced by 'abacus type' bus shelters." And so it remains to this day, the decaying carriage sheds, the goods shed, the weedy expanse of shunting yard and the desolate station area with the Temperance Hotel standing sepulchral guard at its approach, all mute memorials to the junction's busy past.

Thirty five trains a day still stop at the station on the two surviving lines, as compared with twenty two on those lines in 1866, twenty nine in 1886, forty two in 1922 and thirty in 1961. But Craven Arms is now just another place through which the railway passes and at whose station trains stop. The death of the junction – it is one now only in the sense that the railway divides here – has cut the link between the life and economy of the railway and the life and economy of the town. Craven Arms was never a 'railway town' like Crewe or Swindon, with their great engine and carriage works, but it owed its being to its relationship with the railway and that relationship is no more.

The 10.51 Bristol to Liverpool leaving Craven Arms, May 2000

While the fortunes of the railway were changing, so were those of the stockyards. Again the process was gradual and again there were factors outside Craven Arms which drove the change. Although the heavy horse sales dwindled from the 1940s (sales of horses for hunting and riding continued until 1982), the auction yards continued to flourish in the years after the war. In 1960/61 Jackson and McCartney rebuilt the yard at the Smithfield and began store cattle sales on alternate Fridays, sometimes of as many as 1,700 head. And as the 1960s opened they were still advertising their great annual sales of breeding ewes – in 1961 165,000 Clun Forest, Kerry Hill, Speckled Radnor and Cross Bred Ewes and Store Lambs were to be sold in a series of sales from August until the end of October at the firm's yards at Craven Arms, Kington and Knighton. But already the local farming economy was changing. The Kerry Hill breed was becoming less popular; the Shropshire Down of earlier years had gone before the Second World War. And Midland farmers, the buyers of breeding ewes at the great late summer sales, were increasingly turning away from pastoral to arable production. So local farmers, instead of selling their two year old ewes so that others could produce profitable lambs from them, were keeping them to breed the lambs themselves. That brought business to the auction yards, with sales of fat lambs on alternate Mondays at Craven Arms and Ludlow, which were well attended by wholesalers and independent butchers from the West Midlands, but it also spelt the end of the 'largest sheep sale' in England. It passed its centenary in 1974, but by 1980 and the 106th Great Annual Sale, numbers of sheep to be sold were down to 8,000. From then on, as the numbers continued to decline, it was no longer advertised as one in the sequence of annual sales, until in 1985 with only 3,500 sheep for sale there was no mention in the advertising of its being an annual sale. There was also a rationalisation of the two large firms of auctioneers, as Jackson and McCartney amalgamated with Morris, Barker and Poole in January 1968 to become McCartney, Morris and Barker. The centre of gravity of the stock auctions shifted towards the market at Ludlow, the cattle sales going there in October 1994. After McCartneys sold the sites of the cattle pens and of the old horse repository for housing development in 1995, the sole representative of a tradition of great stock sales stretching back to 3 May 1875 is the sale of fat lambs each week on a Wednesday.

Jackson and McCartney's summer sale in the 1960's

The demise of the great sheep sales left the auction field to the north of the Craven Arms Hotel free for alternative use. Onto it went in 1988 the Craven Centre, with its supermarket and cluster of smaller shops and businesses, and later the White Meadow housing development. In concentrating so many shopping outlets under one roof Craven Arms was following a trend which was universal over the country, and as in other parts of the land it had an effect upon the small traders elsewhere in the town. Greater personal mobility which has come, particularly over the last forty years, with the ever increasing private ownership of cars has also affected shopping habits to the detriment of the small local retailer here as elsewhere. As a consequence the centre of gravity of the town's business has moved away from Market Street. Corvedale Road retains businesses as it has done since it began to be built in the late 1870s, but the main focus of shopping lies around and across its junction with the A49.

War memorial in its original position at the corner of Shrewsbury and Corvedale roads

That, in its turn, has exacerbated another of the town's problems – the fact that the principal trunk road along the Welsh border runs through it. This brought advantages for local businesses, like the Agricultural Engineers established by L. P. Morris in the 1940s in Corvedale Road, who use it for distribution of their products up and down the Marches and into Wales. And, so long as the main residential and shopping areas were concentrated upon Corvedale Road, Dale Street, Market Street and Newton Street and there was comparatively little development to the west of the railway, the traffic on the main road was not of pressing concern. That stayed the position until the 1930s, but is no longer the case and has not been for fifty years. Road improvements at the junction by the hotel, such as the removal to Stokesay churchyard in 1956 of the War Memorial

('Old Bill', named after Bruce Bairnsfather's First World War cartoon character), have only scratched at the surface of the problem. The Parish Council first considered the possibility of a bypass running to the east of Craven Arms in June 1953, but the road still cuts the town in two.

That remains a matter for the attention of planners, administrators and councillors. As do the enhancement of support services to match the town's projected growth in housing and the provision of work places to supplement the growth of the industrial estate and light industry which have come in the last decade.

7: CHANGING WITH THE CHANGING TIMES

"Times change, and we change with them" catches the essence of the story of Craven Arms. Down to 1850 the site did not attract a substantial settlement, being but one of the little communities which were scattered over the ecclesiastical parish of Stokesay. This has puzzled some earlier writers who saw the town's location at a meeting of four ways as very suitable for earlier development. In mediaeval times Wistanstow, Corfton, Holgate, Culmington, Clun, Bishop's Castle, Lydbury North and Lydham had all had markets and fairs to serve their local neighbourhoods. By the seventeenth century most of these had ceased and in the early nineteenth only Church Stretton, Much Wenlock, Ludlow, Clun and Bishop's Castle offered markets for the area. Tradition and practice made them the market centre of their neighbourhoods, each some eight to ten miles in radius – the distance, as roads improved, that one could comfortably drive stock or walk in to market and back in a day. Newton lay roughly on the periphery of each of these areas and so time and change, like the main drovers routes out of Wales, passed it by.

The coming of the turnpike roads, with improvements in longer distance travel and carrying, had laid the first seed of change when, at the beginning of the nineteenth century, the Craven Arms Inn was built as a posting house at one of the junctions on the road between Ludlow and Shrewsbury. But for the fifty or so years of the Inn's existence before the railway came it stimulated little change in or development of the life of the immediate neighbourhood. The critical factor was the arrival of the railway, but that alone, like the earlier establishment of the Inn, might not have been enough to trigger the growth of a town, had it not been for another factor. The Inn stood close to the low watershed between the Rivers Onny and Clun which, for the purpose of railway engineering, opened an easy route through the hills which blocked the way westward into Mid-Wales and beyond. And a short distance to the north valleys offered convenient railway routes eastward and north-westward. The creation of the junction drew traffic, trade and business from the surrounding hinterland into the place because of all the advantages of speed, economy and carrying capacity which the burgeoning railway network offered.

In its turn that created the need for and facilitated the growth of a larger settlement both to service the junction and to exploit its economic potential, a process which took some twenty five years to come to full fruition. The first phase of the town's life, then, may be seen as spanning about fifty years. In 1852 the railway arrived. From 1860 to 1870 the junction was developed. From about 1875, with the arrival on the scene of the auctioneers, Rogers and Hamar, the town acquired its stock market, and, as land from the Wolley-Oldnall estate, which was reasonably convenient for the station, came onto the market at about the same time, the town was built and the supporting services developed over the twenty five years down to 1900.

There then followed a period of stability and prosperity. Craven Arms had found its mature role as a junction stock market town. For the next fifty years businesses and families in the natural course of events came and went, but there was a fundamental continuity in both, and, though there was a limited increase in housing in the settlement, the town's character and its function remained essentially unchanged.

By 1950 the railway system across the country was under threat from the growth in the use of motor transport of goods and people both for trade and domestic purposes. The railway junction and its related trade, which outsiders had brought and which had stimulated the birth of the town, was to be taken from it, again by outsiders. As with the creation of the junction, which had taken some twenty years to come into full being, so its decline was spun out over the two decades down to 1970. In the late nineteenth century the town had taken thirty years to come to full life and to fulfil its due role once the junction was in place. So, in the last thirty years of the twentieth century, now that the junction in its fullest sense is no more, the town has had to find and develop a new and different role which will sustain its existence as a viable community. The process of that change is not yet complete. It will be for an historian of the future, perhaps in another fifty years time, to record how it turned out.

INDEX

A49 . . . . 63, 69
Air Gun Club 62
Albion Terrace, Clun Road 36, 37
Aldon .6, 9, 44, 48, 49
Aldon Gutter 6
Aldred, Saxon holder of Stokesay 9
Allcroft family 65
Allcroft, Herbert 39, 42, 43, 44, 62
Allcroft, John Derby 39, 42, 43
Andrews, A. E. of Corvedale Road 59
Ashmore, Miss Victoria 42

Bache, Francis of Rowton 6, 18, 48
Bairnsfather, Bruce 70
Baker, Matthias, map of Manor of Stokesay 15, 32
Baldwyn, Charles of Elsich, and the Baldwyns 11, 12
Barnes, Mr F. W. and the Barnes family 37, 62
Baugh, Robert, map of Shropshire 15
Beambridge 56
Beddoes, Dervies of Whettleton 48
Beddoes, Richard of Rowton 6, 48
Beddoes, Thomas of Cheney Longville 24
Bewick, Miss, teacher at Stokesay Board School 56
Biggs, Richard, guard, of Park Lane 30
Bishop, Herbert of Aldon 48
Bishop's Castle 6, 7, 9, 12, 13, 14, 15, 16, 71
Bishop's Castle Railway 21, 23, 24, 25, 26, 63
Blakeway, Roger 62
Blenheim, house in Shrewsbury Road 50
Brandhill 6, 49
Brassey, Thomas 16, 23, 25
Bright, Reverend John of Totterton 22
Bristol House, Market Street 58
British Restaurant 61
British Legion 61
Bromfield .10, 21
Bromley, Thomas of Step-Aside 48
Brook Road (formerly Gas House Lane) 51, 64

Brown, George H., carpenter and builder 61
Bryn-a-Wel, Clun Road 36
Buckley, Mrs Rosa, M. B. E., midwife 58
Burwarton 11

Cadwallader, Charles, engine driver of Whettleton 30
Cadwallader, Thomas, porter of Whettleton 29, 30
Cadwallader, William, fireman of Culmington 30
Caerleon 8
Callow Hill 6
Carriers' services through Newton Green 14
Catholic Church (St. Andrew's) in Market Street . . .34, 64
Central Wales Railway 23, 25, 67
Chapel, Baptist 42, 46, 61, 63
Chapel, Primitive Methodist 35, 42, 61, 64
Chapel, Wesleyan Methodist 42, 61, 64
Cheshire, John, a joyner 12
Chester, John, parish clerk 52
Chinbaldescote, possibly Dinchope 10
Chukie Chickens .67
Church Stretton 12, 18, 21, 67, 71
Clarke, Ephraim of Towcester 7, 19
Clarke, Gawain, stationmaster 20
Claudius, Emperor of Rome 8
Clifton House, Market Street 35
Clifton, house in Shrewsbury Road 50
Clive, the Honourable R. H. 6, 16, 29
Clun 7, 8, 9, 13, 15, 71
Clun Forest sheep 55, 68
Clun Road 36, 46, 51
Clun Valley 9, 56
Clunbury .10, 62, 66
Coach services through Newton Green 13
Coal merchants at Craven Arms station 21
Condover 21
Corbett, George, lamplighter 49
Corbett, George, postmaster 58
Corfton 71

Corvedale 7, 9, 13
Corvedale Road 33, 34, 46, 51, 64, 69
Coston 10
Coton House 8, 36, 46
Craven Arms Bowls Club 62
Craven Arms Community Centre 66
Craven Arms Cricket Club .62
Craven Arms Fire Brigade .59
Craven Arms Football Club 62
Craven Arms Gas Company 37, 49
Craven Arms Hockey Club .62
Craven Arms Horticultural Show 62
Craven Arms Hotel, Inn . . .5, 7, 15, 39, 44, 50, 54, 63, 71
Craven Arms Male Voice Choir 61
Craven Arms May Fair 60
Craven Arms Men's Chorus 61
Craven Arms Playing Field Association 65
Craven Arms Reading Room and Coffee House Trust 31, 65
Craven Arms station 17, 20, 21, 22, 23, 25, 29, 67, 68
Craven Arms stock markets and sheep sales
. . . . .32, 54, 55, 56, 68, 69
Craven Arms Tennis Club .62
Craven Arms Women's Institute 61
Craven Centre 69
Craven, Dame Elizabeth 11
Craven, Earl of and estate
. . . . .6, 10, 11, 15, 16, 28, 37, 39, 42, 43, 50, 51, 65
Craven House, Shrewsbury Road 51
Craven Lodge, Shrewsbury Road 51
Culmington 71

Dale Street 34, 46, 69
Dale Turkeys, Caynham 67
Dale Villas, Corvedale Road 35
Davies, Thomas, engine driver, Newton Street 35
Davies, David, headmaster Stokesay Board School
. . . . .56, 60, 63
Davies, W., parish councillor 52
Dayus, Charles, veterinary surgeon 36
de Say, Hugh 10, 11
de Say, Picot Lord of Clun 10
de Verdon, John 10
de Lacy, Roger and the Lacy family 10

de Ludlowe, Lawrence and the Ludlow family 11
Deacon, William, of Clunbury school 40
Diddlebury 9
Dinchope 6, 10, 44
Dinmore Tunnel 20
Domesday Book 9, 10, 11
Dorrington 21

Edge, George of Market Street 35
Edge, Thomas, Temperance Hotel Keeper 31, 48
Edge, J. C. and Co. (Bendware) 53, 64
Edgton 10, 13
Edward I 11
Elkes, H. H., parish clerk .52
Empire Day 60
Evacuees 63
Evans, J. of Railway Terrace 59

Farr, Charlie 62
Farrell, George of Milwaukee Terrace 48
Fewtrell, Edward, engine driver of Munslow 30
Finley, George, engine driver 17
Folke, Nurse 58
Forden Gaer, Roman Fort 9
Foresters, Ancient Order of 60
Foster, William, of Railway Terrace 30
Francis, Hayden 62
Frost, Walter, police sergeant 58

Gas House Lane (now Brook Road) 51
Gloucester, Roman road from 8
Gornall, George of Market Street 51
Grange Farm 33, 35
Great Western Railway .25, 51
Green, Joseph, grocer of Newton 46, 48
Green, R. of Knighton 18
Greene, Mr. of Grove estate, Wistanstow 43
Greenfields Road 51, 64
Greensforge, Roman Fort 9
Griffiths, Thomas, guard of Mold 29
Griffiths, W. D., parish councillor 52, 64
Groom, Herbert, farmer 48, 49
The Grove 64, 66

Groves, Thomas, postmaster, Corvedale Road 34, 58
Groves, Mrs Elizabeth, postmistress 58
Gwladys Street Council School, Liverpool 63

Halford 5, 6, 10, 12, 38, 44
Halford Church 60
Halford School 39, 56
Hampstead Marshall 11
Harper, C. of Albion Terrace 59
Hartshorn, Richard 44, 62
Haughmond Abbey 10, 11, 34
Heart of Wales Railway Line 8
Hemmings, Police Constable 61
Hereford, Bishop of 43
Hide, William of Craven Arms Hotel 49
Holgate 71
Hooper, Richard of Railway Terrace 48
Hopesay 9
Horderley 11
Hotchkiss, Henry of Woodville 35, 39, 45
Hotchkiss, Edward of Aldon 35, 39
Hough, John of Dodds Lane 48

Inskip, John of Railway Terrace 30

Jackson and McCartney, auctioneers
..............32, 46, 51, 54, 55, 56, 62, 64, 68, 69
Jellicorse, Rev. William, vicar of Clunbury 40, 43
Jones, John of Grove 26
Jones, Thomas, blacksmith of Newton 34, 35
Jones, G. of Newton 59
Jones, W. of Clun Road 59
Jones, William, postmaster, of Newton, ...58
Jukes, Mrs, teacher at Stokesay Board School 56

Kempton 10, 13
Kennedy, Ivan, headmaster Stokesay Board School .56, 66
Kerry Hill sheep 55, 68
Knighton Railway 23, 25, 29

La Touche, Rev. J. D., vicar of Stokesay .40, 42, 43, 48, 49
La Touche, Miss M. 58
Lambe, George, churchwarden of Stokesay 12

Lambe, Thomas 36, 37, 39
Laurels, Newton Street 35
Leebotwood 16, 21
Leintwardine 9
Leominster 8, 20, 67
Lighting of Craven Arms 49
Lighting and Watching Act 1833 49
Little Woosthidge Field 35, 36
Little Brampton 13, 56
Lloyd, Edward, railway yard foreman of Clungunford ..30
Local Government Board 39, 50
Local Government Act 1894 48
London Midland and Scottish Railway 51
London and North Western Railway 25, 28, 37
Long Lane 6, 12, 13, 15
Long Meadow End 56
Lovatt, George, police sergeant 58
Lucas, A. of Clun Road 59
Ludlow 5, 8, 10, 14, 15, 17, 20, 67, 68, 71
Ludlow Advertiser and Craven Arms Gazette 46
Ludlow District Sanitary Authority 38, 39
Ludlow Gas Company 38
Ludlow Grammar Schools 7, 56
Ludlow Poor Law Union - Board of Guardians 6, 38, 39, 59
Ludlow Rural District Council 39, 50, 51, 67
Lumb, Miss E. E. 30
Lumb, Mrs Emily 31
Lumb, Rev. W. E., vicar of Halford 30, 31
Lydbury North 9, 39, 71
Lydham 71
Lydham Heath 24

McCartney, H. S. 51
McCartney, John 56
McCartney, R. R. and S. W. 65
Magnus-Allcroft, Sir Philip 66
Mail Coach services through Newton Green 13, 14
Market Hall 35, 43, 60, 61, 62, 66
Market Street 34, 46, 69
Marshbrook 9, 16, 21
Marston, Francis of Aston, Hopesay 24
Marston, Richard of Weo 48
Matthews, Matthew, Baptist Minister 42, 43, 48

Maund, A. and Company of Market Street 53
Mayfield Avenue 43, 50
Meadow Road 51
Medlicott, Edward, railwayman 61
Mercia, Kingdom of 9
Midland and Central Wales Junction Railway 24
Midland Waggon Company 24
Milford Haven 23, 24, 25
Miller, W. H., builder of Sibdon View 51
Milwaukee Terrace, Clun Road 36, 37
Mission Church 43, 61, 63, 64
Montgomery 6, 9
Moorwood 6
More, Jasper, M. P. 66
Morgan, John, commodity dealer at Craven Arms . .21, 22
Morgan, Melville, of The Llan, Clunbury 56
Morris, Barker and Poole 55, 56, 69
Morris, Enoch of Stokesay 6, 48
Morris, John, foreman of Gas Works 37
Morris, L. P., Agricultural Engineers 69
Morris, Marshall and Poole, auctioneers 55, 56
Morris, Mary of Newton .29
Mountford, Thomas, headmaster Stokesay School
. . . . .41, 56, 58
Much Wenlock .5, 13, 71
Murray, Nurse 58

Need, James, first keeper of Temperance Hotel 31
New Inn at Newington 15
Newington 6, 9, 12, 13, 37
Newington Estate 64
Newington Terrace 28, 29, 30, 38, 39, 67
Newington Way 51
Newton 6, 7, 10, 12, 15, 19, 29, 37, 45, 46, 48, 66, 71
Newton Club and Feast 59, 60
Newton Green 6, 7, 13, 14
Newton Street .34, 46, 69
Nicholas, William of Manchester House 51
Nicholls, George, engine driver of Chester 29
Noble, Frank 36
Norbury 39, 64
Norton Camp 8
Norton View 39

Oddfellows, Independent order of 60
Offa's Dyke 9
Ogilby's Map 12, 15
"Old Bill" 70
Oldnall, George and family, estate of .6, 28, 33, 35, 50, 71
Onians, Richard .6, 17, 18
Onibury 21
Onnyside Nursing Association 58
Ormsby-Gore, W. 16
Osborne House, Market Street 35
Overend and Gurney, railway financiers 24
Owen, Francis of Newton .7
Owen, William, of Railway Terrace 30
Owens, John of Dale Villas 35

The Paper Shop 35
Park Lane 6, 29
Pearce, William of Onibury 29
Peaton 11
Penlu, Clun Road 36, 46, 60
People's Refreshment House Association 51
Phillips, W., parish councillor 52
Phillips-Wolley, Edward Clive Oldnall Long 33, 34, 35
Pilgrim Centre, Dale Street 42
Plowden, William of Plowden Hall 24
Plymouth Brethren .42, 60
Police in Craven Arms 58, 59
Poor Law Amendment Act 1834 6
Post Offices 45, 58
Post Office, Shrewsbury Road 51, 58
Powell, Roger, Charitable Trust of 6
Powell, George, churchwarden of Stokesay 12
Preece, W. G., auctioneer 45
Presteigne, Clun and Bishop's Castle Railway 24
Price, Thomas, stationmaster 29
Probert, Map of Wolley estate 32, 35
Prospect Place, ...35
Pugh, Richard 37

Railway Terrace 28, 29, 30, 67
Railwaymen's Social Club 61
Railways, projected but not built 24
Read, James Thomas, Temperance Hotel 31, 34

Red Lion, Lion Inn at Newton 7, 15, 42, 44, 45, 60
Reeves, J. of Newton 59
Regal Cinema 53, 66
Reynolds, Roy 62
River Clun 71
River Onny 6, 9, 12, 71
Robertson Honey, Reverend 43
Robertson, Henry, engineer 16, 23
Robinson, Miss Augusta 42
Robson, J.N., proprietor of the Regal Cinema 53
Rogers and Rogers, auctioneers 45
Rogers, George 45, 48, 49
Rogers and Hamar, auctioneers 32, 33, 34, 45, 71
Roman Villa at Craven Arms 9
Romano-British Temple at Craven Arms 9
Rose Cottages 34
Rowton 6, 44, 48

Salmon, Charles of Corvedale Road 48
Salmon, N.of Corvedale Road 59
Savin, Thomas, contractor 23
School Road 33
Sewerage scheme 39
Sheppard, Jeremiah of Whettleton 48
Shrewsbury 5, 7, 9, 11, 12, 13, 14, 71
Shrewsbury and Hereford Railway 5, 16, 18, 19, 22, 24, 25
Shropshire Artillery Band 60
Shropshire County Council 49, 66
Shropshire County Library 66
Shropshire Down sheep 33, 68
Shropshire Mineral Railway 1845 24
Sibdon View, Shrewsbury Road 51
Sibdon Carwood 6, 9, 10, 50
Smith, Gaius (Grocers) of Ludlow 34
Smith, Francis, baker, Corvedale Road 34
Smith, David, butcher, Corvedale Road 34
South Staffordshire and Central Wales Railway 24
South Shropshire Farmers Ltd. 54
Speed, Joseph of Newton Street 48
Spencer, Samuel, timber merchant 54
Spriggins, Mr., landlord of the Red Lion 60
St. Christopher's, Church Youth Club 64
Stanton Lacy 9

Stead, S. of Newton Green 59
Stephens, N., parish councillor 52
Stoke upon Tern 10
Stokesay (Stoke) 5, 6, 7, 9, 38, 39, 44, 49, 50, 59, 71
Stokesay Board School 41, 48, 57, 66
Stokesay Castle 6, 7, 10, 11, 32, 39
Stokesay Castle Farm 8, 12
Stokesay Castle Hotel, Inn 44, 53
Stokesay Church 6, 10, 11, 32, 42
Stokesay National School 32, 40, 41
Stokesay Overseers of the Poor 6, 48
Stokesay Parish Council 39, 48, 59, 63, 65, 67, 70
Stokesay Parish Vestry Meeting 6, 7, 48
Stokesay Parish Workhouse 7
Stokesay Primary School 66
Stokesay Vicarage 32
Street, William, licensee of Red Lion 44
Stretford 8
Stretford Bridge 24
Stubbs and Co.(later Stubbs, Meeson and Co.) 53
Swein, Saxon holder of Clunbury 10

Telford, Thomas 15
Temperance Hall/Hotel 30, 31, 45, 64, 65, 68
Temperance movement 30
Terry, C. of Newton Street 59
Thomas, Mrs, teacher at Stokesay Board School 56
Thomas, Edwin, postmaster 58
Thursfield, Doctor, Medical Officer of Health ..38, 39, 57
Tithe Apportionment Map 1840 ....15, 32
Toll gates 13
Tomlins, James, miller of Snead 22
Torr, Albert, guard of Slapton, Devon 29, 61
Tredinnick, Doctor Ernest 36, 57, 60, 62
Tumpy Field 8
Turnpike Acts 13

View Edge 6, 8

Walker, John, stationmaster 18, 19, 20
Water mains, provision of 39, 50
Watling Street 6, 8, 9, 13
Wenlock Railway Act 1861 and Railway 24, 67

Weo 48
Weyman, Thomas of Purslow Hall 24
Whettleton 6, 8, 10, 12, 44, 48
Whettleton Common 6, 60
Whettleton Pool 6, 13
White Meadow Close 64, 69
Wightman, Mrs Julia 30
Williams, Thomas, farmer of Montgomery 22
Williams, Mrs Mary, midwife 58
Wilson, Rev. T. P. 30
Wilton House, Corvedale Road 35
Wilton Lodge, Clun Road 36, 46
Windsor Clive, Lord and Lady 39
Wistanstow 6, 9, 13, 17, 71
Wolley, Thomas and family, estate of 33, 35, 50, 71
Wood, C. P. 64
Wood, J. P. and Sons, London House, Market St. .64, 66, 67
Woodhouse, Sir Michael 12
Woodville, Clun Road 35
Wooferton 20
Wroxeter 8

Yew Tree Cottage, Newton Street 35